ALSO BY MARY GORDON

READING
JESUS

READING JESUS

A Writer's Encounter with the Gospels

Mary Gordon

PANTHEON BOOKS
NEW YORK

Grateful acknowledgment is made to the following for permission
to reprint previously published material:

Harvard University Press: "I dwell in possibility" and "Renunciation is a piercing virtue"
from The Poems of Emily Dickinson, edited by Thomas H. Johnson, copyright © 1951,
1955, 1979, 1983 by the President and Fellows of Harvard College (Cambridge, Mass.:
The Belknap Press of Harvard University Press). Reprinted by permission of
Harvard University Press and the Trustees of Amherst College.

New Directions Publishing Corp.: Excerpts from "St. Thomas Didymus"
from A Door in the Hive by Denise Levertov, copyright © 1989 by Denise Levertov.
Reprinted by permission of New Directions Publishing Corp.

Oxford University Press: Excerpt from "The Habit of Perfection"
from Poems by Gerard Manley Hopkins (New York: Oxford University Press, 1970).
Reprinted by permission of Oxford University Press, on behalf of The British
Province of the Society of Jesus.

Library of Congress Cataloging-in-Publication Data
Gordon, Mary, [date]-
Reading Jesus : a writer's encounter with the
Gospels / Mary Gordon.
p. cm.
ISBN 978-0-375-42457-1
1. Jesus Christ—Person and offices.   2. Bible. N.T.
Gospels—Criticism, interpretation, etc.   I. Title.
BT205.G67 2009
232—dc22
2009004975

www.pantheonbooks.com

Book design by Maggie Hinders

Printed in the United States of America

First Edition

2 4 6 8 9 7 5 3 1

For my son, David, who seeks

Contents

III

The Seven Last Words and the Last Words

I dwell in Possibility—
A fairer House than Prose—
More numerous of Windows—
Superior—for Doors—

Of Chambers as the Cedars—
Impregnable of Eye—
And for an Everlasting Roof
The Gambrels of the Sky—

Of Visitors—the fairest—
For Occupation—This—
The spreading wide my narrow Hands
To gather Paradise—

—EMILY DICKINSON

"INSTEAD of giving a firm foundation for setting the conscience of man at rest forever, Thou didst choose all that is exceptional, vague and enigmatic."

—FYODOR DOSTOYEVSKY, *The Brothers Karamazov*

I AM IN A NEW YORK CITY TAXI. It is rush hour, and the traffic is at a standstill: even the slightest movement has no chance of taking place. The driver, an African American whom I take to be in his sixties—he has a neatly clipped silvery moustache and is wearing a gray tweed cap—turns on the radio. I hear the voice of a religious broadcaster—the tone itself makes me uneasy—the misapprehended, mislearned overelegance that takes the polish of an older age, a polish that, when well done, inspired confidence, and turns it stentorian. Instead of feeling secure, as I did when I heard the voice of Edward R. Murrow or Walter Cronkite, I am on my guard. I'm going to be sold something, and the product is inferior: a car I don't want, with a new paint job and shiny grillwork and an engine that will break down on the highway at midnight, leaving me stranded, in danger, and alone. More: there seems to be something slightly sexually perverse in the unctuousness—as if I were about to be kidnapped and will find myself, awake after a drug-induced coma, in involuntary servitude in a brothel in one of the world's hot, damp, historically failed colonial outposts. The broadcaster is talking about Jesus. "Pick up your book," he says, "and read the words along with me."

Then he begins speaking, or rather, shouting, about how at the end of the world Jesus will come in fire, separating the sheep from the goats. He is literally quoting chapter and verse: Matthew 25:31–33.

They happen to be chapters and verses I'm familiar with—the words, that is; I wouldn't have known the numbers. He moves from quotation to interpretation. The goats are homosexuals, abortionists, divorcées.

It isn't call-in radio, but if it were I would say, "Wait a minute, Reverend . . . that chapter, those verses, don't say anything about homosexuals, abortionists, and divorcées. Jesus is talking about people who will not feed the hungry. Pick up your book, Reverend, and read."

The radio voice bids his listeners farewell, and he blesses them in the name of the Lord. Then I hear another voice, announcing a new program: an interview with a member of something called the Full Gospel Business Men's Fellowships.

I hear the words "Full Gospel." My first response is distaste for the juxtaposition of the words "Gospel" and "Businessmen." But then it occurs to me, with a clutch of anxiety and shame, that I have never actually read the full Gospel—which is not really one Gospel, but four: four accounts of the life of Jesus written by four different writers, Matthew, Mark, Luke, and John—that I have almost reached the age of sixty and never had the readerly experience of beginning with the first words of Matthew and continuing through to the Last Words of John.

Brought up as a Roman Catholic in the 1950s, I did not grow up reading the Bible. We weren't forbidden Scriptural reading, but it was certainly discouraged: that was something Protestants did. Protestants, who didn't realize the danger of individual interpretation, the rich safety of ex cathedra pronouncements, worked out by a body of ordained men over centuries of inspired time.

And so, I didn't read the Gospels. Rather, I heard the portions of them that were read out from the pulpit each Sunday. This was a singular way of knowing a text: fragmented, chopped up, interpreted before I had a chance really to digest what the words had said. And yet I have always been able to say with certainty that the figure of Jesus and the words of Jesus have been at the center of my ethical and religious imagination. This struck me, suddenly, as very strange indeed.

I jumped out of the taxi with an urgency and a generosity of tipping that must have astonished, if not alarmed, my driver. I was going to read the Gospel. Or the Gospels. Right then, straight through, and not get up till I was done.

It was a disturbing and exhilarating enterprise, with the particular disturbance and exhilaration that has always marked my sense that I am being seized by a new subject: a demand that I experience as a deep hunger to write. But what would I write? About what? And to whom? And how?

One way of going about it would be to write *against* something, to write aggressively, defensively. I did find the interpretation of the radio broadcaster and the Full Gospel Business Men distressing, threatening, even dangerous. I could imagine myself writing to protect my treasure—*my parables, my Beatitudes, my Last Supper, my Crucifixion story*—those Gospel passages that had, almost before memory began, in Virginia Woolf's words, incised themselves in the soft wax at the base of my spine. I have felt threatened, as if I were in danger of being stolen from. Because what is being done in the name of Jesus seems to me a betrayal of everything that I understand the Gospels to be about.

But the impulse to write in order to correct, humiliate, or punish, while it can focus the mind like the prospect of a hanging, subjects the same mind to a requisite narrowness. Too much remains unregarded. Certainly, I could say that Fundamentalists read the way they did because they were wicked and stupid, willful distorters of Jesus' teachings. But that did not seem to me the absolutely best approach. While this would provide the thrill of the slammed door, it would also close off light and the sound of voices. How, I wondered, could I begin in a place where both I and the radio preacher could meet?

The place is the place of reading. But even if we are standing in the same place, the place of reading, we see and hear different things when we lift our eyes and incline our ears. The Fundamentalists have made the text an idol; before them is a golden calf; surrounding me a violent wind, rushing. And in the distance, barely audible, a still small voice.

I AM VERY USED TO conversations among writers, full of lamentations that our culture is no longer made up primarily of people who think of themselves as readers. But the radio preacher and his audience are the kind of devoted readers that writers like me long for and only dream of. They read, and they reread. They know the text more thoroughly than people like me, who think of ourselves as living for literature, know any text, even the ones to which we devote ourselves, professionally or for plain love. The radio preacher and his audience are the new people of the book.

When they read the Gospels, they say that they are reading the Gospels. When I read the Gospels, I say that I am reading the Gospels. And yet I find their readings so different from mine, it is difficult for me to believe that we are doing the same thing, that one word, "reading," is adequate to describe these very different experiences.

But is this reading intrinsically different from other enterprises called reading? The Gospels are made up of words, written by human

beings, a narrative about the life of Jesus. But who is Jesus, this character who is known, most importantly, through words?

It seemed to me, then, that if I were going to take this project seriously, I would have to question my own reading, and examine its lacu-
nae: I would have to ask myself, do I really know what the Gospels are
about, or have I invented a Jesus to fulfill my own wishes? Can I really
say what the difference is between Matthew, Mark, Luke, and John,
as books, in the way that I can describe the difference between a novel
by Trollope and a novel by Dickens?

And if the Gospels are a book, I began to wonder, how is it possible to explain or describe the kind of book they might be? Why are
there four Gospels, and four authors, all recounting the story of one
person's life? All creating a character with the same name: Jesus. Why
is there not just one Gospel, one version of this life, credited to a single
author, or with no author named, like the Book of Judges or the Book
of Kings? Or why not a hundred Gospels? Who decided, and how
did this canonized text come to be? I had no idea.

I went to the library to try to find out. It came as something of a
relief to me to discover that no one really knows.

The New Testament scholar Bruce Metzger says, "Nothing is
more amazing in the annals of the Christian church than the absence
of detailed accounts of so significant a process."*

I learned that the final canonization of the twenty-seven books of
the New Testament was not completed until A.D. 367, three centuries
after the first Gospel (Mark's) was written, around the year 65.
Matthew's and Luke's Gospels are thought to have been composed
around 70 or 80; John's is the latest, probably around the year 90.

---

* Bruce Metzger, *The Canon of the New Testament* (Oxford: Clarendon Press, 1997).

They were compilations of oral histories set down a full generation or more after the death of Jesus. No one suggests that these words were set down by Jesus himself. As the great New Testament scholar Raymond Brown notes, "Unlike Moses, who by tradition authored the Pentateuch, Jesus did not produce a writing that contained his revelation. He is never recorded as setting down even a word in his lifetime or telling any of his disciples to write. Accordingly, the proclamation of the kingdom of God made present in Jesus did not depend on writing."*

I learned, too, that the editorial decisions that resulted in the Gospels as we know them were the result of the labor of many hands whose work went on for centuries. The decisions were made on grounds of doctrinal orthodoxy; many Gospels, prominent among which are those known as the Gnostic Gospels, were rejected on these grounds. The Gospels of Matthew, Mark, and Luke (called the synoptic Gospels because they contain quite similar material) and that of John were authorized on the grounds that these authors alone were either apostles (Matthew and John) or the companions of apostles (Mark, who supposedly accompanied Peter, and Luke, supposedly a kind of secretary to Paul). One of the most influential editors, Irenaeus, Bishop of Lyons, insisted in the year 180 that there were four and only four Gospels because there are four zones of the world, four principal winds, and that the cherubim have four faces.†

But all Christians read like editors, holding in our hands a pencil that we do not fear to use whenever we see fit. Perhaps it is more true

---

* Raymond E. Brown, *An Introduction to the New Testament* (New York: Doubleday, 1997), p. 5.
† Harry Gamble, *The New Testament Canon* (Philadelphia: Fortress Press, 1985), p. 314.

to say: all Christians are bowdlerizers. When we come to something we cannot or will not accept, we skip over it, hoping to find something we are happy to hold on to in the next chapter, the next verse, the next page, the next Evangelist.

Perhaps the most famous and audacious bowdlerizer of the New Testament is Thomas Jefferson. He simply took out all the parts of the New Testament he didn't like and put together his own. As a recreation from the pressures of the presidency, he took a pair of scissors to the editions of the New Testament in the four languages he knew—English, French, Latin, and Greek—reconstituting the Gospels so they would be a force for good. And not just generalized good: he was particular in his intentions. The original title of his compilation was "The Philosophy of Jesus of Nazareth, extracted from the account of his life and doctrines, as given by Matthew, Mark, Luke and John; being an Abridgement of the New Testament for use of the Indians, unembarrassed with matters of faith or fact beyond the level of their comprehensions."

He had the enviable certainty of an Enlightenment thinker. He knew what were really the words of Jesus and which were not. How could he tell? Well, it was obvious. He could tell. After all, wasn't he the author of the words "We hold these truths to be self-evident"? With the same faith, he wrote to John Adams, "We must reduce our volume to the simple Evangelists, select, even from among them, the very words only of Jesus, pairing off the amphiboligisms into which they have been led, by forgetting often, or not understanding, what had fallen from him, by giving their own misconceptions of his dicta, and expressing unintelligibly for others what they had not understood themselves. There will be found remaining the most sublime and benevolent code of morals which has ever been offered to man. I have performed this operation for my own use, by cutting verse by verse out of the printed book, and arranging the matter which is evidently his and which is as easily distinguished as diamonds in a dung hill."*

It would not be difficult for me to explain the difference between Jefferson's reading and mine: it would be odd if a gap of two hundred fifty years didn't produce a different set of preferences and priorities. But how can I explain the radical gap between my reading of the Gospels and that of my contemporaries who insist on a reading as different from mine as Jefferson's was from Irenaeus'? Why don't I feel compelled by literalism, why can I tolerate contradiction and ambiguity in a way that they cannot? The difference must be explained, in part, by the kind of reading I have learned to do as a writer and reader of literary texts.

I can only imagine that the impulse to what I call Fundamentalism is motivated by an anxious desire to hold on to words that you imagine cannot and will not change. This anxiety is infinitely understandable. There is certainly, in this world, much to fear. Disease, terrorism, the degradation of the planet. A global economy that no one seems to understand, that seems entirely out of control. An epistemic whirligig that makes old certainties about the continuity of the self and the relationship to the past and to time seem newly up for grabs. For many people, questions about sexual behavior and sexual identity are a cause for terror as real as Al Qaeda. That this brand of terror does not animate most of the people who write the kind of books I write and read is neither here nor there. What is not in

---

* Bruce Braden, ed., "*Ye Will Say I Am No Christian*": *The Thomas Jefferson/John Adams Correspondence on Religion, Morals, and Values* (Amherst, N.Y.: Prometheus Books, 2006), pp. 99–100.

doubt is the climate of fear that seeps into the fabric of global consciousness—most particularly for Americans, who are, arguably, the safest, healthiest, most prosperous people in history.

When I try to understand a flavor of fear I do not share, the impulse that produces traditional hellfire-and-brimstone preaching and even the more contemporary don't-worry-be-happy versions, I imagine that people who are in its grip feel the way I do when I'm experiencing turbulence on an airplane. At these moments, the fact that many people are not troubled by turbulence is of no moment to me. When I feel the plane bucking, I want reassurance. I don't really care whether or not the reassurance is based on fact. I want a pilot, whom I can imagine to be blue-eyed, with a silvery crew cut, getting on the microphone and saying, "Don't worry, everyone, I know what's causing the turbulence, and I'll make sure we're nowhere near it." Or: "The turbulence is nothing; we'll have an on-time landing at JFK."

When I'm gripping my seat with one hand and clutching the sleeve of a perfect stranger with the other, I don't want to hear, "Hi, folks, I'm hoping we'll make a safe landing, I'm quite well trained, and the airplane is a fine machine, but if there's a computer glitch or a wind shear, there's nothing I can do." Imagining what I would feel if I heard these words when I was in turbulence, I speculate that this is what some people experience when they hear someone, whom they think of as a religious authority, saying, "We don't have the answers for everything. There are some things that cannot be explained. The good suffer, children die grotesquely, earthquakes and tsunamis destroy thousands in a second, the evil prosper, and we cannot tell you why. But we can give you lots of historical and linguistic context."

And so, when I decided finally to embark upon this project I imagined myself on a turbulent plane ride, flying in the dark. I have no notion that I am the pilot, rather a combination flight attendant and tour guide. I see myself walking up the aisle, navigating what I am pleased to call the refreshment cart in challenging four-inch stilettos. I am wearing a uniform designed by Givenchy or Yves Saint Laurent, or perhaps the classic blue-gray Pan Am stewardess uniform of my childhood. I am saying, "Look out the window with me. This is what I see . . . I'd like you to see it with me. Turbulence is the ordinary; turbulence is our lot. I have no idea where we're landing, or if it will be on time."

I am trying for a tone that is personal and self-questioning. I am looking for a Jesus among specific words. Believing, because of my history as a reader and a writer, that he is a character—unique in his impact on the history of the race but nevertheless a character, someone who is known to us primarily through a text. A text that is a narrative. It is for this reason that I am excluding the Epistles attributed to Paul from this study. The Epistles are theology, interpretative, and I, as a writer of narrative, prefer to focus on the way Jesus is made known through narrative. As someone whose actions and gestures are described in words in order that he might be known by a reader. My colleague at Barnard College, Professor Randall Balmer, an expert on Evangelical and fundamentalist religion, has pointed out to me that most Evangelicals and Fundamentalists are much more drawn to Paul and the Old Testament than the Gospels. They prefer the certainty of law and prescription to the fluidity of narrative.

I imagine objections from those who will tell me that the Gospels are not words written by human beings only, but words written by human beings under divine inspiration. At the same time, I fear the accusation of Scriptural scholars that my reading of the Gospels without understanding historical and linguistic contexts is naïve to the point of irresponsibility. That it is a deliberate and aggressive anti-intellectual stance. I prefer to think that, alongside my deep respect and gratitude for the work of Biblical scholars, I can place the hope that there is room for work like mine next to theirs, if only because most of the people in the world who have read the Bible have not had access to this scholarship. Prominent among the imagined passengers on my turbulent flight is Sky Masterson, the hero of *Guys and Dolls,* who saves the Salvation Army Mission because he knows the Bible backward and forward—as a result of having spent so many nights in hotel rooms where the Gideons always provided him with reading material. They did not, however, provide him with scholarly commentary.

And, by necessity, Biblical scholars have avoided tones of strong emotion. But the Evangelicals have jumped into that breach, hurtling toward their own agenda. So I feel free to speak not with the voice of scholarly authority, but with a writer's voice. I am striving for a tone and diction that neither shouts nor threatens, a diction that neither promises falsely, nor underestimates the power of fear, or supposes that, with right thinking, it can be brought under control. Above all, I have no interest in making a doctrinal point, no desire to convert—a word whose roots are in the Latin word for "turn"—I have no desire that, reading what I have written, anyone will turn to or turn away from anything. I assume that many of the people who read me, like most of my friends and colleagues, a large proportion of the people I love, are not people who have a relationship to Jesus that has anything to do with faith. "Poetry makes nothing happen," W. H. Auden famously said, and I have always believed that, for the kind of writer I am, any other position is a delusion or a danger.

. . .

I WOULD VENTURE TO say I have no method, to say nothing of a methodology. I have consulted works of theology, Christology, Scriptural studies . . . but mostly I have read and reread and reread the Gospels. In five different translations, including the King James, the New Revised Standard, the New English, and the New American Bible. When I focused on various passages, I settled on whatever translation has the most resonance for me in the particular instance. Nothing but an accident of tonality drove my selection process; the reader looking for consistency will, I fear, be disappointed.

My most singular readings occurred when I used my family Bible. The Douay-Rheims version: an attempt by English Catholics exiled from their native land to create an alternative to the King James. So in looking for passages, I would come across the record of my own birth in my father's handwriting, my recording of his death as a child trying for her best penmanship, as well as my two marriages, the births of my two children, my mother's death, my daughter's marriage. The nature of this book—a text available to anyone who chose to buy it, and yet entirely unique as it contains the handwriting of my beloved dead and marks the important moments of my life—is a perfect metaphor for the particular qualities, the particular problems that face anyone who is trying to write about "Scripture." When is a book not a book? When it is the Bible. But, if it's not a book, what is it? Because after all, it's something to read. And so my method is simply a method of reading and rereading. An attempt at openness, a hope that I will be enlightened, shocked, surprised.

I want to read the Gospels in a way that relates to these words of Simone Weil: "Our thought should be in relation to all particular and already formulated thoughts, as a man on a mountain who, as he looks forward, sees also below him, without actually looking at them, a great many forests and plains. Above all our thought should be empty, waiting, not seeking anything, but ready to receive in its naked truth the object that is to penetrate it."*

This is an impossible project, and in that it is impossible, I feel drawn to it. To this task of adding my voice—personal, formed importantly by words—to the many voices who have spoken so many words about the words for which people have lived and died and killed and been killed.

---

* Simone Weil, *The Simone Weil Reader* (New York: David McKay Co., 1977), p. 49.

I

These Fragments
I Have Shored
Against My Ruins

I AM UNEASY CALLING MYSELF A PERSON OF FAITH, if faith is seen as a synonym for certainty, or even an unwavering trust in what I know. I cannot recognize in myself an essential stability that quickly rights itself after the occasional brief faltering or stumble. Many days, there seems no possibility that there is any kind of reality corresponding to or behind the word "God." I know that I have often been mistaken, often proven wrong, including and especially about matters that I would once have called "articles of faith," matters that I once believed I had to believe under pain of damnation, an eternity in a hell I took to be literal and real. I am ready, therefore, at any time to learn that almost everything and anything I know is wrong, or at least in need of radical revision.

And yet I could never say of myself, "I am not a person of faith," because I know that I am different from people who do not have a religious imagination. I am drawn to a sense of ultimate meaningfulness, even though I can only apprehend it dimly: a figure in a mist, a shape on the horizon. That shape, that figure, embodies itself in a person, Jesus, whom I came to know through the words of the Gospel.

The elusiveness of the figure, its essential ungraspableness, leads me to the understanding that the kind of person of faith I am is a person of hopeful faith. Hope is the vector that pulls me toward the irresistible incomprehensible. And yet the ungraspable, the incomprehensible, is nevertheless rooted in profound attachments. I feel this attachment when I am praying in a place with others, possibly radically different from me in race, class, education, background . . . all of us saying the same words, the same words that people have said for a thousand years.

My faith, grounded in attachments and fueled by hope, whose symbol is a flaming heart, is mobile, motile, with the mobility and the motility corresponding to the age in which I was born. Yet I am not unrooted. What keeps me from flying off, or apart? Why do I know myself with a particular clarity as a person of faith when I read a best-selling attack on the idea of God, an attack that seems vulgarly ahistorical, intellectually crude? Why do I resist as insufficient the postmodern ironic default setting whose favorite form is parody, and whose preferred task is unmasking? It is clear to me that I prefer the risky question found in Eliot's *The Waste Land*: "What are the roots that clutch, what branches grow / out of this stony rubbish? Son of man, / you cannot say, or guess, for you know only / a heap of broken images."

For one thing the terms are more resonant; for another, more would seem to be at stake.

It is nearly a hundred years since Eliot wrote those words, and the passage of time makes the word "only" seem less crucial. A heap of broken images seems like quite a precious cargo, quite a desirable patrimony. A place to stand. A place to which one can become attached.

And so, as I said, I am a person of attachments. My attachments are not to a set of ideas but to a series of images and tones. Images and tones that resonate, like the tone of a foghorn or the lighthouse beam, indicating something, suggesting something, a something apprehended not exactly by the mind, as if they were a series of directions to be followed, but by the animal's directed sense.

Image. Tone. Gesture. Phrase. Scene. Fragments.

. . .

"THESE FRAGMENTS I have shored against my ruins." These words from Eliot's *Waste Land* involved me in an interesting misreading that went on for several decades. I had habitually misread the plural "ruins" as the singular "ruin." I was shocked to find out what I had done, and not pleased with Eliot's words: I preferred my own invention. I had interpreted the line to mean that the words were a preservation against personal ruin. But "ruins" suggests a public spectacle—like the Parthenon or the Acropolis—and what would be the point of shoring fragments against these colossal wrecks? Such an act becomes an act of witness rather than of self-preservation.

But whatever Eliot meant or I understood, I came to know Jesus in fragments. Not Jesus, whom I would never have called Jesus (that was for Protestants, with their impulse to soften or democratize), but Christ. Before this enterprise of reading the Gospels straight through, beginning to end, Matthew to John, my understanding of them, therefore of their subject, Jesus, came to me in fragments. Fragments that I heard—the Gospel read by the priest from the altar at Mass (during my childhood the only English words I would have heard in the course of the Mass prayers)—then read, as I followed the priest's voice in the missal I was given for my eighth birthday.

Alongside the words, though, there were visual images, part of my life from earliest memory. Images on the walls of the house I lived in, the houses of everyone I knew. Pictures in books, read to me as I sat on my father's lap, later the subject of my first experience of reading. But, in the Catholic world of the triumphalist fifties, sacred images were popularized, commercialized: we had puzzles, coloring books, sticker books, pencil cases, lunch boxes, dish towels, saltcellars, dinner plates. We colored the sacred, ate off it, dried our dishes with it, carried it in our purses and our book bags, reached for it at lunch or at our desks.

But these sacred images don't restrict themselves to the ones absorbed in childhood. Along with my childhood puzzle of Jesus and the children is Bellini's risen Christ, and Fra Angelico's, Dostoyevski's tempted Jesus and Pasolini's enraged reformer. Not only my life but the life of a culture, the history of a civilization. Called Christian. After Jesus Christ.

AND SO, if no reading is innocent, how singularly un-innocent is my reading of the Gospels? I bring to it, simply, my life. Information, mis-information, garblings, elisions, words that told me who I was and others that made me know what I would never be.

Where to begin such a reading? Perhaps with the memory, the image, that seems to have been with me before memory can fix a time.

The Prodigal Son.

1

The Running Father,
the Starving Son,
the Fatted Calf,
the Husks,
the Unbearable Question

Then Jesus said, "There was a man who had two sons. The younger of them said to his father, 'Father, give me the share of the property that will belong to me.' So he divided his property between them. A few days later the younger son gathered all he had and traveled to a distant country, and there he squandered his property in dissolute living. When he had spent everything, a severe famine took place throughout that country, and he began to be in need. So he went and hired himself out to one of the citizens of that country, who sent him to the field to feed the pigs. He would gladly have filled himself with the husks that the pigs were eating; and no one gave him anything. But when he came to himself he said, 'How many of my father's hired hands have bread enough and to spare, but I am dying of hunger! I will get up and go to my father, and I will say to him, "Father, I have sinned against heaven and before you; I am no longer worthy to be called your son; treat me like one of your hired hands."' So he set off and went to his father. But while he was still far off, his father saw him and was filled with compassion; he ran and put his arms around him and kissed him. Then the son said to him, 'Father, I have sinned against heaven and before you; I am no longer worthy to be called your son.' But the father said to his slaves, 'Quickly, bring out a robe—the best one—and put it on him; put a ring on his finger and sandals on his feet. And get the fatted calf and kill it, and let us eat and celebrate; for this son of mine was dead and is alive again; he was lost and is found!' And they began to celebrate.

"Now his elder son was in the field; and when he came and approached the house, he heard music and dancing. He called one of the slaves and asked what was going on. He replied, 'Your brother has come, and your father has killed the fatted calf, because he has got him back safe and sound.' Then he became angry and refused to go in. His father came out and began to plead with him. But he answered his father, 'Listen! For all these years I have been working like a slave for you, and I have never disobeyed your command; yet you have never given me even a young goat so that I might celebrate with my friends. But when this son of yours came back, who has devoured your property with prostitutes, you killed the fatted calf for him!' Then the father said to him, 'Son, you are always with me, and all that is mine is yours. But we had to celebrate and rejoice, because this brother of yours was dead and has come to life; he was lost and has been found.' " LUKE 15:11–32

"For the kingdom of heaven is like a landowner who went out early in the morning to hire laborers for his vineyard. After agreeing with the laborers for the usual daily wage, he sent them into his vineyard. When he went out about nine o'clock, he saw others standing idle in the marketplace; and he said to them, 'You also go into the vineyard, and I will pay you whatever is right.' So they went. When he went out again about noon and about three o'clock, he did the same. And about five o'clock he went out and found others standing around; and he said to them, 'Why are you standing here idle all day?' They said to him, 'Because no one has hired us.' He said to them, 'You also go into the vineyard.' When evening came, the owner of the vineyard said to his manager, 'Call the laborers and give them their pay, beginning with the last and then going to the first.' When those hired about five o'clock came, each of them received the usual daily wage. Now when the first came, they thought they would receive more; but each of them also received the usual daily wage. And when they received it, they grumbled against the landowner, saying, 'These last worked only one hour, and you have made them equal to us who have borne the burden of the day and the scorching heat.' But he replied to one of them, 'Friend, I am doing you no wrong; did you not agree with me for the usual daily wage? Take what belongs to you and go; I choose to give to this last the same as I give to you. Am I not allowed to do what I choose with what belongs to me? Or are you envious because I am generous?' So the last will be first, and the first will be last."

MATTHEW 20:1–16

Is it possible that the story of the Prodigal Son is the first story I remember? Or that I remember it alongside Snow White, Goldilocks, the Three Little Pigs? Fixing it in my mind (they weren't wrong, the iconoclasts; they knew the power of artifacts) was one of my most treasured possessions, what we would now call a sticker book. At that time what are now called stickers were referred to as "seals," the model being Easter Seals, which you bought in order to pledge your determination to stamp out polio. They were not common, these books of seals, and certainly a book of Bible stories was not. I can recall the taste of the glue on my tongue—sharp, cutting, even painful— and the drastic importance to me of the correct placement of the sticky image onto the blank square that was meant to frame it.

The seal of the Prodigal Son presented him bare-chested among the pigs. But in my imagination, I created other costumes for him: the robe, which I saw very clearly. It was striped, magenta, orange, red. And the ring, a large signet ring that I knew went on his index finger, although I had never seen anyone in life wear any jewelry on that digit. I saw his legs, smooth, tanned (was I confusing him with the Old Testament Jacob, as I confused his robe with Joseph's many-colored coat?). But there were other images that were more vivid to me than these, images that I felt kinesthetically rather than saw. The first were the husks provided for the pigs; he longed for the husks, envied the pigs: even husks had not been provided for him. I imagined used-up corncobs, tossed on the ground after a summer picnic. Dried out; devoid of succulence. I understood that he would have to wait even for these until the pigs had had their fill; without articulating it, I knew that he was less valuable to his employer than the pigs were. This frightened me: that kind of hunger.

I was the child of an ardent father, so I could imagine the heat of a father's embrace that was led up to by a yearning run: the unseemly speed of the father who could not wait to see his child. Who runs for him, unable to bear the slowness of the normal progression, the son's ordinary pace. I could feel the warmth of the father's ardent arms; I knew the boy's safety, his sense of relief. Forgiveness. From a very young age, I understood that there was much for which I needed to be forgiven, although this was an abstract category, because in life as I lived it, any offenses I committed were minor. Nevertheless, I was terrified by the sound of two words, "reform school." I knew something could happen, some policeman somewhere would see through the carapace of my customary good behavior and take me from my home to some place of banishment, punishment, that my wastrel ways had earned. To be released from that sentence, to the arms of the father— I could not then, and cannot now, imagine a more desirable fate than this.

THIS STORY IS ONE of the most important reasons that I can think of myself as a follower of Jesus, despite many good reasons not to be. Jesus made up this story, and although Raymond Brown has reminded us that Jesus is not a writer, he is a creator of fictions. Everything in the story came from his mind, as everything in every story I have written, everything in the fictions of the writers I love, Chekhov, Flaubert, Proust, Virginia Woolf, comes from theirs. I approach the Prodigal Son now as a person who has spent her life reading and writing fictions. And from that perspective, I find it the perfect story. It contains all the elements required of a story if it is to satisfy and move. From the first words, we are presented with a situation compelling in its terms and complications. The pacing is rhythmical, dramatic; the details thicken the situation; the difficulties increase, until the final end which leaves us at a party, rather than a place of neat resolution.

Of the four Evangelists, only Luke presents it. Luke, the most domestic, the most poetic, the most contemplative of the four. It is the third of three parables that speak of the importance of recovering loss. The first is the parable of the lost sheep, which makes the point that the good shepherd searches for his lost sheep, and treasures the lost one the most dearly. The second parable of the series, the woman and the lost coin, tells the story of a poor woman who sweeps her house, searching desperately for a lost coin, and focuses on her joy when she at last recovers it. It is a response to an accusation of the Pharisees and scribes, "This fellow welcomes sinners and eats with them."

We are told that there is a father, and he has two sons. The younger son wants his money, now. We know this will lead to no good. We doubt the father's wisdom, granting such a heedless wish. Had he said no to his young son, the boy would have been forced to stay at home and share the sensible location, the prudent placement of the elder brother.

But the father says yes. Thus far there are only shadows, traces or hints of characters. The father and his greedy son. Of the older son we as yet know nothing.

We follow the fate of the younger son. He shoots his wad. He blows it on whores. Of the three characters who will populate the story, the youngest son is the least completely drawn, and in a way we know him least: he remains of the three most a type, least a character. A spoiled boy—we aren't even convinced of the sincerity of his apologies to his father. He plans his words in advance; first we hear him rehearsing them, and then repeating them in his father's actual presence. The father's emotions are named; he is "filled with compassion."

We know the elder son's emotional state; he is angry. But the boy—he seems to have the lack of self-consciousness of the irresponsible user.

The father has not much interest in the apology. It is something that has to be said, something to be got through. It is certainly not something that makes possible what follows it.

As a child, and as a young person, I paid no attention to the older son. If you had asked me, I would not have been able to tell you that he had a place in a story. The young are prodigal; providence is a virtue of the middle-aged. I have gone from being heedless to being careful: I have become much more the son who never left home and worked hard than the traveling boy, the squanderer. And so, reading it recently, my heart goes out to the older brother. Of course he is outraged; his sense of justice has been thrown into a cocked hat. He has worked hard for his father; his brother has run away and squandered everything in a particularly disreputable way. And what has he earned for his good behavior? Not even a goat. Certainly not a party. His father has betrayed him, and he responds to his father with what is usually the child's first ethical statement, "It's not fair."

A great deal is at stake with this unsettling story. Suppose it says that loyalty counts for nothing? Suppose love is unearnable, unearned? Suppose instead of a situation of rights, there is an economy of grace? Suppose it is unfathomable, as divorced from the rational as the impulse that sends the father running to meet his child on the road? That animal impulse, that full of the heat of blood? Suppose that life is larger, odder, less predictable, and more surprising than we had thought or even hoped. Particularly those of us who by the very virtue of reading this particular example of English prose are more likely to be descendents of the careful brother than the prodigal?

"Everything I have is yours." The good boy is not left bereft. But what has been lost has been found. What is acknowledged here, what is given the greatest weight, is the terrible blow of loss. The loss that has seemed final, and then: reprieve. Resurrection. A new chance. A rebirth whose wage is celebration. "We had to celebrate and rejoice." Had to: an injunction, a duty. The duty of celebration. In King James: "It was meet that we should make merry."

And the story ends here. With an assertion of the rightness of celebration. The propriety of joy.

But what of justice? The difficulty of accepting an economy of mercy is echoed in the parable of the vineyard, which recounts the incident of a landlord who pays the same wages to workers who have worked all day as to those who have worked only an hour. When the workers complain, they are greeted with the question "Are you envious because I am generous?"

It is an impossible question, calling for an impossible honesty, one that makes self-love nearly impossible. The answer: yes. I am envious because you are generous. I am envious because my work has not been rewarded. I am envious because someone got away with something. Envy has eaten out my heart.

It is to me one of the most ethically complex, therefore greatest questions ever presented. A question with no answer. A circle without a break. Except the break of mercy, the break of grace.

But why, then, should we strive, why should we give our best, our all? Does this kind of striving only lead to envy?

The radical challenge of Jesus: perhaps everything we think in order to know ourselves as comfortable citizens of a predictable world is wrong.

And then how do we live?

In celebration.

Without envy.

Generously.

And justice? What is to become of that?

It is easy to focus on the potential narcissism of an insistence upon justice if one is not being oppressed by the unjust. But what of justice for the victims? Isn't mercy another excuse for noblesse oblige rather than an assertion of the primacy of human rights? Isn't it better that there should be some clearly stated measure, some setting out of obligations, some recourse to law . . . a law which can be enforced or abrogated, but is stable, within reach for consultation and recourse? We are given, instead, two sentences, each in its way unbearable.

"Are you envious because I am generous?"

"Everything I have is yours."

But we are creatures of outsize appetites, and sometimes when we hear "everything," our response is: "Not enough."

2

Swine

When he came to the other side, to the country of the Gadarenes, two demoniacs coming out of the tombs met him. They were so fierce that no one could pass that way. Suddenly they shouted, "What have you to do with us, Son of God? Have you come here to torment us before the time?" Now a large herd of swine was feeding at some distance from them. The demons begged him, "If you cast us out, send us into the herd of swine." And he said to them, "Go!" So they came out and entered the swine; and suddenly, the whole herd rushed down the steep bank into the sea and perished in the water.   MATTHEW 8:28–32

❧

They came to the other side of the sea, to the country of the Gerasenes. And when he had stepped out of the boat, immediately a man out of the tombs with an unclean spirit met him. He lived among the tombs; and no one could restrain him any more, even with a chain; for he had been restrained with shackles and chains, but the chains he wrenched apart, and the shackles he broke in pieces; and no one had the strength to subdue him.

Night and day among the tombs and on the mountains he was always howling and bruising himself with stones. When he saw Jesus from a distance, he ran and bowed down before him; and he shouted at the top of his voice, "What have you to do with me, Jesus, Son of the Most High God? I adjure you by God, do not torment me." For he had said to him, "Come out of the man, you unclean spirit." Then Jesus asked him, "What is your name?" He replied, "My name is Legion; for we are many." He begged him earnestly not to send them out of the country. Now there on the hillside a great herd of swine was feeding; and the unclean spirits begged him, "Send us into the swine; let us enter them." So he gave them permission. And the unclean spirits came out and entered the swine; and the herd, numbering about two thousand, rushed down the steep bank into the sea, and were drowned in the sea. MARK 5:1–13

❧

Then they arrived at the country of the Gerasenes, which is opposite Galilee. As he stepped out on land, a man of the city who had demons met him. For a long time he had worn no clothes, and he did not live in a house but in the tombs. When he saw Jesus, he fell down before him and shouted at the top of his voice, "What have you to do with me, Jesus, son of the Most High God? I beg you, do not torment me"—for Jesus had commanded the unclean spirit to come out of the man. (For many times it had seized him; he was kept under guard and bound with chains and shackles, but he would break the bonds and be driven by the demon into the wilds.) Jesus then asked him, "What is your name?" He said, "Legion"; for many demons had entered him. They begged him not to order them to go back into the abyss.

Now there on the hillside a large herd of swine was feeding; and the demons begged Jesus to let them enter these. So he gave them permission. Then the demons came out of the man and entered the swine, and the herd rushed down the steep bank into the lake and was drowned. LUKE 8:26–33

IN THE CHARACTER OF THE DEMONIAC, one of the figures most threatening to civilized people is evoked. The man possessed; the one who has lost himself. Lost himself to what? To where? Who is in charge of him; who is in control? Matthew says there are two of them, and gives us very little detail; from Mark and Luke we have a composite picture of abjection, pathos, horror. The demoniac lives among the tombs: has he been banished or is he self-banishing? Whatever the case, his home is among the dead. He is like the dead or like an animal: he howls, he does not wear clothing, he does not have a house. He is wild. Savage. Like an animal, he must be chained—for his protection or the protection of the community? This is not made clear. What could be more frightening—the naked man, howling among the dead, gashing himself with stones, sometimes disappearing into the wilderness: his wildness unbearable even to himself.

How should he be categorized: as one of the dead, or as an animal? We are always frightened by the liminal: the liminal is unsusceptible to language, one of whose major functions is to distinguish. The mad make us feel helpless and frightened because they do not use language in the way *we* do; their use of language makes them a *they*—no bridging the gulf between the sensible and those beyond sense.

Enclosed in his wretched body: the dark, unbridled force of destructive energy. With the power to break chains and shackles— and what else? Our bones? Our houses? The force civilization can do nothing with; the force that makes a joke of the power of the Word.

But the demons and Jesus speak the same language. They recognize him. He and they are able to have a conversation. They supplicate; they bargain. "Do not torment us . . . do not banish us to the abyss." They would prefer not to leave the wretched man—or is it that they would prefer not to be bereft of him? To be separated from one's victims, at the moment of banishment, is to contemplate an emptiness. They have been companions on the journey to wretchedness. To uncouple oneself from the living is always to lose.

"Do not banish us to the abyss." The demons utter our most heartfelt cry: Do not force me to be nothing. To be completely abandoned. In a place—the abyss—where there is nothing to distinguish, or to grasp. Do not consign us to nothingness.

Before he will grant their request, Jesus must know their name. They tell him their name: "Legion." What a strange answer, legion, a Roman term, a military term. A large body of fighting soldiers: an organized killing machine.

"Send us into the swine. Let us enter there." What does it mean that a lodgment in the body of an unclean, more, a doomed animal is less terrifying than the abyss? Is the nothing always our greatest fear?

Jesus takes the forces of wildness, of destruction, and makes them susceptible to language, to reason. He civilizes them. He does something with them. What does he make of them? Drowned swine. The scene we do not see: two thousand pigs, drowned. In King James: choked.

But what does it mean, this form of animal sacrifice? What does it say about the nature of human destructive force? Must animals pay the price? Because it must go somewhere, this dark power.

If they are a metaphor, for what do they stand?

What surplus do they represent? What expendable flesh?

The mystery of the requirement of expendable flesh.

The relief of the prospect of expendable flesh if that is what is required to civilize the darkness.

When the demoniac, clean now, and clothed, asks to follow Jesus, Jesus refuses. Go home, he says, tell everyone what happened.

To what home did he go?

And later, how did he receive the news of the Resurrection? Or did it seem to him old news, since he himself had been delivered from the dead? Returned, like the promise of resurrection, to the land of the living. By the power of the Word. A conversation with the demons.

3

The Burning Tongue,
the Barren Womb

And following Him was a large crowd of the people, and of women who were mourning and lamenting Him. But Jesus turning to them said, "Daughters of Jerusalem, stop weeping for Me, but weep for yourselves and for your children. For behold, the days are coming when they will say, 'Blessed are the barren, and the wombs that never bore, and the breasts that never nursed.' Then they will begin to say to the mountains, 'Fall on us,' and to the hills, 'Cover us.' For if they do these things when the tree is green, what will happen when it is dry?" LUKE 23:27–31

❦

"There was a rich man who was dressed in purple and fine linen and lived in luxury every day. At his gate was laid a beggar named Lazarus, covered with sores and longing to eat what fell from the rich man's table. Even the dogs came and licked his sores. The time came when the beggar died and the angels carried him to Abraham's side. The rich man also died and was buried. In Hell, where he was in torment, he looked up and saw

Abraham far away, with Lazarus by his side. So he called to him, 'Father Abraham, have pity on me and send Lazarus to dip the tip of his finger in water and cool my tongue, because I am in agony in this fire.' But Abraham replied, 'Son, remember that in your lifetime you received your good things, while Lazarus received bad things, but now he is comforted here and you are in agony. And besides all this, between us and you a great chasm has been fixed, so that those who want to go from here to you cannot, nor can anyone cross over from there to us.' He answered, 'Then I beg you, Father, send Lazarus to my father's house, for I have five brothers. Let him warn them, so that they will not also come to this place of torment.' Abraham replied, 'They have Moses and the Prophets; let them listen to them.' 'No, Father Abraham,' he said, 'but if someone from the dead goes to them, they will repent.' He said to him, 'If they do not listen to Moses and the Prophets, they will not be convinced even if someone rises from the dead.' " LUKE 16:19–31

HEARING, AS I DID, the words of Jesus from my earliest memory, there are things that I have always known: that money is a problem, and that there may be times when it is right to long for death. As a child, this made me very different from the Americans I was growing up among. They feared Communists or kidnappers; what I feared was larger, more elusive, more pervasive, and therefore less susceptible to containment or control.

The words of Jesus do not offer consolation if by consolation you mean the assurance that the worst will not happen, or will not happen to you. A substantial percentage of his language is apocalyptic; when I heard it, I thought the time frame applied to me; it didn't occur to me that those listening to Jesus thought it applied to their lifetimes, that Jesus might have thought that as well. It wasn't hard to be apocalyptic when, each week, you and your classmates were ordered under your desks for air-raid drills, in case of an atomic bomb. I have always wondered who imagined that being under a school desk would be a real protection against nuclear attack. Clearly, what was important was the gesture, and the whipping up of fear.

So we were afraid, all of us, of literally going up in flames. It was easy to imagine a horror so unbearable that one would wish to be crushed by a mountain. "And if that is said in a green wood, what about the dry?" What could be more terrible than wishing to be crushed by a mountain? Jesus suggests a terribleness beyond our imagination.

But the words of Jesus to the women of Jerusalem, spoken as he is carrying his cross on the way to his death, personalized the fear, domesticated it, and made it less the stuff of horror movie, more of individual tragedy. He is saying to the women: The worst can happen to you, and there will be nothing you can do about it, and it will not be your fault. It is the consolation of a man condemned, a consolation that reminds us we are, all of us, condemned. For at the best, we are condemned to the end of life, and at the worst, to what he is going through: physical pain, betrayal, disgrace.

But what has always moved me most about Jesus' sympathy for the women of Jerusalem, even as he approaches his own horror, is the instance of a male mind imaging disaster in female terms. Before I had children, I understood it as a figure of speech: things will be so terrible, it will be better not to have little ones under your charge. All the women I knew said that having children was their greatest joy; so I understood Jesus to be saying that that which is dearest to you would be most painful to lose, to watch destroyed. But when I had children, those words froze my heart. What mother has not prayed, "Spare my child." What mother has not bargained with God, "I will suffer anything, torture, long illness, loss of everything, but spare my child." Of all sorrows, to watch the suffering of a child is for a mother the worst. Which of the classical writers wrote, "Better it is not to have been born?" It is easier to say that about oneself than about one's progeny. To say it about oneself limits the horror to one's own particular biography; to say that the very phenomenon of giving birth is a tragedy widens the focus immeasurably. With these words, Jesus articulates a particularly female fear, even as he is going to his death.

So we feared the flames of the atomic bomb, but we also feared the flames of hell. There was a kind of priest, often a visiting missionary, who specialized in evoking terrifying details. He was explicit about the various agonies that would befall the body, maintaining that the greatest agony was separation from God, but the eternal stink of burning flesh, the sizzle of fat and skin and tendon—these were much more real to us than the idea of separation, which we figured we could handle if the time came.

This kind of priest was also eloquent about the eternal thirst that was the portion of the damned. This was something I could imagine clearly; I was often thirsty as a child. In my experience, children are thirstier than adults, perhaps because they're shorter and it's harder for them to get to the sources that could alleviate their thirst. I have clear memories of waking in the night, the word "parched" a somatic reality as my tongue stuck to my palate. And being outdoors, not allowed to go inside—"Go and play, it's nice out"—on a steaming summer day, longing for water as the only imaginable good.

It was very easy for me to call up this physical memory when the parable of the rich man and Lazarus was read aloud at Mass. I was absolutely present when the rich man begs Lazarus "to wet his finger to cool his burning tongue." And it was easy for me to understand the rich man's sin; his was the sin of arrogant privilege. Every day he passed by Lazarus, who sat at his door, and the dogs licked his sores. I could never figure out if the dogs licking his sores made things better or worse for him; sometimes I thought it might be soothing, sometimes I understood it as the low point of abjection.

The rich man's sin is not only a failure to share his wealth, but equally important, a failure of attention. What he has done in his past life, where he is going after he leaves Lazarus, are of no concern to Jesus. He doesn't seem like the worst person in the world: he's not cruel or dishonest or hypocritical. He just doesn't see.

This parable expresses the essential genius of Christian charity: that it must be personal, personalized. It has nothing to do with duty;

it is the opposite of philanthropy. Philanthropy allows for acts of charity that keep the recipient at a distance. Giving to Oxfam, the Red Cross, to Mother Teresa's sisters, we might receive a photograph of a leper. But the leper does not appear at our threshold. Our beloved canine friends are not in the business of licking sores.

For Jesus, what is required is an encounter. What is insisted upon is the personal responsibility of love. Jesus demands of Peter, "Who do you say I am?" When he reports what others have said, Jesus isn't satisfied. He repeats, "But who do *you* say I am?"

And at the end of Matthew's Gospel, Jesus insists upon the grounds of salvation and damnation in the clearest possible terms, and the terms are personal:

> "I was hungry and you gave me food, I was thirsty and you gave me something to drink, I was a stranger and you welcomed me, I was naked and you gave me clothing, I was sick and you took care of me, I was in prison and you visited me." Then the righteous will answer him, "Lord, when was it that we saw you hungry and gave you food, or thirsty and gave you something to drink? And when was it that we saw you a stranger and welcomed you, or naked and gave you clothing? And when was it that we saw you sick or in prison and visited you?" And the king will answer them, "Truly I tell you, just as you did it to one of the least of these who are members of my family, you did it to me." . . . "You that are accursed, depart from me into the eternal fire prepared for the devil and his angels; for I was hungry and you gave me no food, I was thirsty and you gave me nothing to drink, I was a stranger and you did not welcome me, naked and you did not give me cloth-

ing, sick and in prison and you did not visit me." Then they also will answer, "Lord, when was it that we saw you hungry or thirsty or a stranger or naked or sick or in prison, and did not take care of you?" Then he will answer them, "Truly I tell you, just as you did not do it to one of the least of these, you did not do it to me." And these will go away into eternal punishment, but the righteous into eternal life.   MATTHEW 25:35–46

Humans will be saved or damned, then, based on behavior which begins with acts of faulty or correct perception . . . a comprehension that the poor and the needy are in fact Jesus himself.

It seems clear to me that the parable of the rich man and Lazarus insists upon what Catholic liberation theologians call "the preferential option for the poor." Even the way the characters are named favors Lazarus. The rich man is nameless in most translations. In the Latin Vulgate, he is called Dives, which is generic for "a rich man," whereas Lazarus is named by Jesus. Lazarus means "God will help."

As a child, beggars frightened me, but I used to force myself to look at them, and to give them money; the more unattractive, the more pushing they were, the more important it seemed to me to respond to them. For many years when I took the subway with my father, we would see a man at the Lexington Avenue subway station. He was covered with sores; he held in his filthy hand a filthy paper cup. And I was afraid to look at him. When I didn't look at him, I remembered Dives, and I made myself look, and I always gave him money. But I was afraid that was not enough, and when the time came, he would not wet his fingertip to cool my tongue. Because I knew that he was Lazarus, and I was clearly in a position more like Dives' than like his.

Even now I read the parable as a warning: it is right we should fear punishment for what we do not see. And the day will come when the bill falls due. But my anxiety does not seem to affect the kind of Christian who identifies himself with the Gospel of Prosperity, whose focus seems to be on the prosperity of the believer rather than on the needs of the poor. Inevitably, the suggestion arises that the poor are poor because of some fault of their own, because their connection to God is weak, or garbled. The Prosperity Gospel preachers pay lip service to the responsibility to share one's God-given wealth. But they don't notice that it is only the impoverished Lazarus who is in Abraham's bosom, and the rich don't seem to be taking up residency in that particularly desirable real estate.

"If someone rose from the dead, they still would not believe him." Only now I notice the ironic end. The weary, almost hopeless leader suggesting the unlikeliness of his mission's success. The improbability of the power of faith. For believing Christians, the event of someone's rising from the dead has indeed occurred. And we do not, as a species, as a clutch of individuals, seem to be behaving any better.

As a child, I didn't notice the irony, the weariness. I was only scared. Now, my fear has an extra layer: the fear of human paralysis. I hear an echo of the moment in Conrad's *The Secret Agent* when the anarchist drops into a pit of utter despair because he thinks not even the detonation of a bomb will rouse the London populace. "What if nothing could move them?" he says.

As always, I am unsure if Jesus is articulating my worst fears, or if his words create or at least feed them.

4

Perfume,
Hair

Now when Jesus was in Bethany, in the house of Simon the leper, there came unto him a woman having an alabaster box of very precious ointment, and poured it on his head, as he sat at meat. But when his disciples saw it, they had indignation, saying, "To what purpose is this waste? For the ointment might have been sold for much, and given to the poor." When Jesus understood it, he said unto them, "Why trouble ye the woman? for she hath wrought a good work upon me. For ye have the poor always with you; but me ye have not always. For in that she hath poured this ointment on my body, she did it for my burial. Verily I say unto you, Wheresoever this gospel shall be preached in the whole world, there shall also this, that this woman hath done, be told for a memorial of her." Then one of the twelve, called Judas Iscariot, went unto the chief priests, and said unto them, "What will ye give me, and I will deliver him unto you?" And they covenanted with him for thirty pieces of silver. And from that time he sought opportunity to betray him. MATTHEW 26:6–16

And being in Bethany in the house of Simon the leper, as he sat at meat, there came a woman having an alabaster box of ointment of spikenard very precious; and she brake the box, and poured it on his head. And there were some that had indignation within themselves, and said, "Why was this waste of ointment made? For it might have been sold for more than three hundred pence, and have been given to the poor." And they murmured against her. And Jesus said, "Let her alone; why trouble ye her? She hath wrought a good work on me. For ye have the poor with you always, and whensoever ye will ye may do them good; but me ye have not always. She hath done what she could; she is come aforehand to anoint my body to the burying. Verily I say unto you, Wheresover this gospel shall be preached throughout the whole world, this also that she hath done shall be spoken of for a memorial of her." And Judas Iscariot, one of the twelve, went unto the chief priests, to betray him unto them.

MARK 14:3–10

❧

And one of the Pharisees desired him that he would eat with him. And he went into the Pharisee's house, and sat down to meat. And, behold, a woman in the city, which was a sinner, when she knew that Jesus sat at meat in the Pharisee's house, brought an alabaster box of ointment, and stood at his feet behind him weeping, and began to wash his feet with tears, and did wipe them with the hairs of her head, and kissed his feet, and anointed them with the ointment. Now when the Pharisee which had bidden him saw it, he spake within himself saying, "This man, if he were a prophet, would have known who and what manner of woman this is that toucheth him: for she is a sinner." And Jesus answering said unto him, "Simon, I have somewhat to say unto thee." And he saith, "Master, say on." "There was a certain creditor which had two debtors; the one owed five hundred pence, and the other fifty. And when they had nothing to pay, he frankly forgave them both. Tell me therefore, which of them will love him most." Simon answered and said, "I suppose that he, to whom he forgave most." And he said unto him, "Thou has rightly judged." And he turned to the woman, and said unto Simon, "Seest thou this woman? I entered into thine house, thou gavest me no water for my feet; but she hath washed my feet with tears, and wiped them with the hairs of her head. Thou gavest me no kiss; but this woman since the time I came in hath not ceased to kiss my feet. My head with oil thou didst not anoint, but this woman hath anointed my feet with ointment. Wherefore I say unto thee, Her sins, which are many, are forgiven; for she loved much; but to whom little is forgiven, the same loveth little." And he said unto her, "Thy sins are forgiven."

And they that sat at meat with him began to say within themselves, "Who is this that forgiveth sins also?"

And he said to the woman, "Thy faith has saved thee, go in peace."   LUKE 7:36–50

❧

Then Jesus six days before the Passover came to Bethany, where Lazarus was which had been dead, whom he raised from the dead. There they made him a supper; and Martha served; but

Lazarus was one of them that sat at the table with him. Then took Mary a pound of ointment of spikenard, very costly, and anointed the feet of Jesus and wiped his feet with her hair; and the house was filled with the odor of the ointment. Then saith one of his disciples, Judas Iscariot, Simon's son, which should betray him, "Why was not this ointment sold for three hundred pence, and given to the poor?" This he said, not that he cared for the poor; but because he was a thief, and had the bag, and bare what was put therein. Then said Jesus, "Let her alone; against the day of my burying hath she kept this. For the poor always ye have with you; but me ye have not always." JOHN 12:1–8

ALL FOUR EVANGELISTS tell the story: something about a woman and perfume—but the similarities end there. And the differences have contributed to an odd conflation so that the story of the washing of Jesus' feet by Mary ties itself, in the minds of people who hear it, into a colorful knot of confused details.

Matthew and Mark don't give any identification to the woman; for Luke, she is a sinner, for John, the sister of Martha and Lazarus. Both Luke and John name her as one kind of outsider woman: the nondomestic. Harlot or contemplative; in either case she is fit to be no man's wife. In Matthew and Mark, Jesus promises her a place in history. But we are not told her name.

In Mark, Jesus says of the woman, "She has done what she could." This is a remarkable sentence. Mostly, when we say it, it is a kind of lie; we mean to defend ourselves; we mean exactly the opposite. "I did what I could" usually means, "There was more I could have done but I didn't do it." What a rare thing it is, to have done what one could. What one can. To do the thing that calls out to be done, if only one is attentive, ready. Attentiveness, readiness; Jesus is clear on the importance of these.

Luke's version of the woman washing Jesus' feet is the most anomalous of the four. Usually counted among the synoptics, in that he is understood to be working from the same sources as Matthew and Mark, Luke in his treatment of this event radically stands out from his brothers. For one thing, unlike the other versions, this one occurs relatively near the beginning, in the seventh chapter, less than halfway through. He does not include the phrase "the poor you always have with you"; his purpose is not to point out the financial hypocrisy of the just. In the other versions, this story occurs just prior to the main events of the Passion narrative; it is seen as providing Judas' immediate motivation for betraying Christ. This has always made me sympathize with Judas; the moralist's dismay at the teacher's going back on his clear word, the man who lives by justice unable to loosen the ties of his rigidities. I think of a certain kind of Marxist who fears beauty as a capitalist snare.

The tone of those words—the poor you always have with you—must have felt like a slap in the face. They are extraordinarily harsh, indifferent to human suffering, suggesting, rather than advocacy of the poor, an aristocratic coldness reminiscent of Talleyrand's response to the beggar who opportuned him, saying, "Sir I must live." "I do not see the necessity for that," Talleyrand responded.

Judas is not mentioned in Luke's version; he uses the incident as another moment to stress the importance of forgiveness.

And only Luke uses the word "love." He uses it twice: once to make it clear that forgiving a really advanced sinner is a good investment: the greater the forgiveness, the greater the return of love. Later, Jesus says that the woman's sins have been forgiven, "for she loved much."

An act of extravagance wiping out years of bad behavior. Once again, Jesus undercuts the careful, the provident, the steady—in favor of something unquantifiable, incomprehensible, something that fits under the heading of the word "love."

This woman brings out the chivalric in Jesus; he becomes the chevalier of Gerard Manley Hopkins's poem "The Windhover." He defends the woman against the accusations of the moral bullies. "Leave her alone, why do you trouble her?" he says in Mark, and in Matthew, "Why trouble her, she has performed a good service upon me." Luke goes furthest: Jesus insults his host, a Pharisee (in Matthew and Mark the host is Simon the leper; in John the hosts are Martha, Mary, and Lazarus), for not being as attentive as the woman. The headlong woman's dream: a strong man to say to her critics, "Leave her alone." And they obey.

FEET. TEARS. PERFUME. HAIR. The story is saturated with sexuality, and visual artists have luxuriated in the iconography. It is the most purely sensual moment in the Gospels. John notes that "the house was filled with the fragrance of the perfume." I heard the word "nard," and later, "spikenard," and although I had no idea what the precise odor might be, it called up for me the idea of Middle Eastern preciousness: the exotic, something of the casbah, the harem—both of which words I knew mainly from movies of dark men and veiled women doing unspeakable things the likes of which we Catholics wouldn't even know the names of. It was much later that I learned it was a generic term for any kind of precious fragrance; it might have been something like lavender, something like valerian. Later still that I read of Horace offering Virgil a whole barrel of his best wine in exchange for a phial of nard.

But what really gripped me was Mary washing Jesus' feet with her tears and wiping his feet with her hair. I thought how enviably long and lush such hair might be; thick, spread, useful—no one I had ever seen had hair like that. I understood that such a failure was a failure of the modern to provide what my imagination went to older ages for. Washing someone's feet with your tears and drying them with your hair. It's an extreme act, almost embarrassing. As a child, I was a little uneasy at the display inherent in this story, the clear sensuality, and perhaps I was jealous of Mary, a pride of place, a special attention granted her because of her beautiful hair.

The other references to hair in the Gospel are to John the Baptist wearing a coat of camel's hair, or God counting the hairs on everyone's head. Not a hint that hair would be a vehicle of beauty or allure. But this is a moment for the body's enjoyment; refreshment—even as that refreshment is a prophecy of death.

THIS IS A SHOCKING STORY; it provides various flavors of shock. My girlish shock at Jesus' sensuality was replaced later by an ethical shock engendered by the words "the poor you always have with you." The radical egalitarian who says that no one should claim pride of place upbraids his host for insufficient attention paid to him, for his failures in hospitality. . . . Jesus, the ascetic who keeps warning his followers against the lures and snares of money and what it buys, who in the previous chapter of Matthew separates the saved from the damned on the basis of their generosity to the poor, says that it is the right thing not to sell a luxury item to feed the hungry. The concept of waste, essential to any aesthete. "Waste not, want not" was not a sentence written by an artist.

And it is as an artist that this story is most important to me. Because in the moment of the washing of the feet, Jesus insists that beauty matters: that the aesthetic can take precedence over the moral. Tormented as I have always been by the vision of myself as Dives stepping over the sore-covered Lazurus to get, not to a feast, but to my writing desk, I have been comforted and assured by imagining myself the purchaser of nard, the lover with the spreading hair. Because in this story love wins over duty, passion and the body's joys eclipse justice.

Or it could be read as justifying disregard for the needs of the suffering poor. Who are always with us. Who never go away.

But Jesus doesn't say, "Forget about them." Rather, he reminds us that along with our responsibilities, there is the necessity of respite. The animal's replenishment. The Sabbath of the skin.

5

A Dream of Whiteness

Jesus took with him Peter and James and his brother John and led them up a high mountain, by themselves. And he was transfigured before them, and his face shone like the sun, and his clothes became dazzling white. Suddenly there appeared to them Moses and Elijah, talking with him. Then Peter said to Jesus, "Lord, it is good for us to be here; if you wish, I will make three dwellings here, one for you, one for Moses, and one for Elijah." While he was still speaking, suddenly a bright cloud overshadowed them, and from the cloud a voice said, "This is my son, the Beloved; with him I am well pleased. Listen to him!" When the disciples heard this, they fell to the ground and were overcome by fear. But Jesus came and touched them, saying, "Get up and do not be afraid." And when they looked up, they saw no one except Jesus himself alone. MATTHEW 17:1–8

❧

Jesus took with him Peter and James and John, and led them up a high mountain apart, by themselves. And he was transfigured before them, and his clothes became dazzling white, such as no one on earth could bleach them. And there appeared to them Elijah with Moses who were talking with Jesus. Then Peter said to Jesus, "Rabbi, it is good for us to be here; let us make three dwellings, one for you, one for Moses, and one for Elijah." He did not know what to say, for they were terrified. Then a cloud overshadowed them, and from the cloud there came a voice, "This is my Son, the Beloved, listen to him!" Suddenly when they looked around, they saw no one with them any more, but only Jesus. MARK 9:2–8

❧

Jesus took with him Peter and John and James, and went up on the mountain to pray. And while he was praying, the appearance of his face changed, and his clothes became dazzling white. Suddenly they saw two men, Moses and Elijah, talking to him. They appeared in glory and were speaking of his departure, which he was about to accomplish at Jerusalem. Now Peter and his companions were weighed down with sleep; but since they had stayed awake, they saw his glory and the two men who stood with him. Just as they were leaving him, Peter said to Jesus, "Master, it is good for us to be here; let us make three dwellings, one for you, one for Moses, and one for Elijah"—not knowing what he said. While he was saying this, a cloud came and overshadowed them; and they were terrified as they entered the cloud. Then from the cloud came a voice that said, "This is my son, my Chosen; listen to him!" When the voice had spoken, Jesus was found alone. LUKE 9:28–36

AN INCIDENT OF WHITENESS.

Radiant, irradiated.

What is the meaning of this moment? I heard the story for many years, probably well into adulthood, before I thought to question the sense of the word "transfiguration." Some of my cousins lived in a parish in Brooklyn called Transfiguration. In the way of those times, the sacred word was made ordinary. "Where do you go to school?" "Transfiguration." "God, we have to play Transfiguration next week. They're the division champs."

Transfiguration. It is more, or less, than transformation. The figure—the *figura*—is changed, not only the form. The *figura*, the face, the bearer of individuality, identity. A difference more radical, more permanent than transformation. But when I heard the word, its import was not intellectual. It was aesthetic, not about a human life or an event in history. Its subject was light, light and shadow. Whistler could paint it: monochrome.

The lure of illumination. The lure of the luminous. We are creatures drawn to light. To be illuminated is to be under the illusion that the flesh is light; gravityless; will not bring us down.

The splendor of the luminous.

"Splendor." "Glory." What do these words mean? They have something to do with power, and with the acknowledgment and naming of that power. They have to do with visibility, a combination of beauty, visibility, renown. They have to do with being impressive, with making an impression. They are connected in the common mind with riches, or at least expense. Their context in nature would seem to do with the sun or the stars—an important light source. "Glory" can be used pejoratively, to suggest excessive pride, boastfulness. Boasting to whom? Glory happens publicly . . . an excess of visibility.

IN THIS STORY, the moment ceases being purely visible, the silence is broken, the white silence, by the voice in the cloud. Fear enters with language.

Peter says he will build three dwellings. But nothing comes of it. He says it not knowing what he says. He is expressing the human impulse to do something in the face of the ineffable, the beauty that overwhelms. Past speech, past action, too. He is speaking out of fear. A workman's chattering. As is often the case with Peter, he doesn't get it. His mind is scrambled, perhaps, by the fear of being overshadowed; the fear of the cloud.

A whiteness whiter than the greatest bleacher. Coveted whiteness: labor intensive, precious, and hard won. The problem of whiteness as a category in the history of humankind.

What is white? Snow, stars, the moon.

Luke says, "His face was white as lightning."

To present a face transfigured by language is the writer's task.

Also to bring the past (Moses, Elijah) and the present (Jesus, the disciples) together in a moment utterly alive. Moses, the only human ever to have seen God (though from the rear), and Elijah, the only human not to have experienced ordinary death, stand in the same place as Jesus and the disciples. The glorious past of the Jewish people is made literally present at this moment in Jesus' ministry.

· · ·

AT THIS MOMENT Jesus insists upon being seen. And so it can be read as the celebration of the visible.

But it is a singular mode of seeing. A seeing by God the father, a seeing which results in being named the Chosen, the Beloved. A seeing accompanied by the insistence that Jesus be listened to.

The apex of the desirable.

The New English Bible translates the words of God: "This is my beloved son in whom I take delight." So we are in the presence of delight. Delight as an aspect of the holy.

And Jesus tells them to say nothing. After this experience of bedazzlement, there is the adjuration to keep silent.

And then they come down the mountain.

I WANDERED ONCE by chance into a Catholic church in San Francisco where the Mass was being said half in Chinese, and half in English. The priest, who was Chinese, preached on the Transfiguration. "We don't know whether this really happened," he said, "but if it did, it was one of those moments where the veil between the invisible and the visible is torn away." He spoke of a mentally handicapped man with whom he worked. When he asked the man if he prayed, the man said he did, and when he prayed, what he meant was that he listened. The priest asked what he heard. The man said, "I hear: 'You are my beloved.'" The priest told the congregation, "This is what we should always be hearing."

6

The Dark Garden

Then cometh Jesus with them unto a place called Gethesmene, and saith unto the disciples, "Sit ye here, while I go and pray yonder." And he took with him Peter and the two sons of Zebedee, and began to be sorrowful and very heavy. Then saith he unto them, "My soul is exceeding sorrowful, even unto death: tarry ye here, and watch with me." And he went a little further, and fell on his face, and prayed, saying, "O my Father, if it be possible, let this cup pass from me: nevertheless not as I will, but as thou wilt." And he cometh unto the disciples, and findeth them asleep and saith unto Peter, "What, could ye not watch with me one hour? Watch and pray, that ye enter not into temptation: the spirit indeed is willing, but the flesh is weak."

He went away again the second time, and prayed, saying, "O my Father, if this cup may not pass away from me, except I drink it, thy will be done." And he came and found them asleep again: for their eyes were heavy. And he left them, and went away again, and prayed the third time, saying the same words.

Then cometh he to his disciples, and saith unto them, "Sleep on now, and take your rest; behold, the hour is at hand, and the

43

Son of man is betrayed into the hands of sinners. Rise, let us be going: behold, he is at hand that doth betray me." And while he yet spake, lo, Judas, one of the twelve, came, and with him a great multitude with swords and staves, from the chief priests and elders of the people. Now he that betrayed him gave them a sign, saying, "Whomsoever I shall kiss, that same is he; hold him fast."

And forthwith he came to Jesus, and said, "Hail, master"; and kissed him. And Jesus said unto him, "Friend, wherefore art thou come?" Then came they, and laid hands on Jesus, and took him.

And, behold, one of them which were with Jesus stretched out his hand, and drew his sword, and struck a servant of the high priest's, and smote off his ear. Then said Jesus unto him, "Put up again thy sword into its place, for all they that take the sword shall perish with the sword. Thinkest thou that I cannot now pray to my Father, and he shall presently give me more than twelve legions of angels? But how then shall the scriptures be fulfilled, that thus it must be?"

In that same hour said Jesus to the multitudes, "Are ye come out as against a thief with swords and staves for to take me? I sat daily with you teaching in the temple, and ye laid no hold on me."

But all this was done, that the scriptures of the prophets might be fulfilled. Then all the disciples forsook him, and fled. And they that had laid hold on Jesus led him away to Caiaphas the high priest, where the scribes and elders were assembled.

MATTHEW 26:36–57

And they came to a place which was named Gethsemane; and he saith to his disciples, "Sit ye here, while I shall pray." And he taketh with him Peter and James and John, and began to be sore amazed, and to be very heavy; and saith unto them, "My soul is exceeding sorrowful unto death; tarry ye here, and watch." And he went forward a little, and fell on the ground, and prayed that, if it were possible, the hour might pass from him. And he said, "Abba, Father, all things are possible unto thee; take away this cup from me; nevertheless not what I will, but what thou wilt."

And he cometh, and findeth them sleeping, and saith unto Peter, "Simon, sleepest thou? Couldst not thou watch one hour? Watch ye and pray, lest ye enter into temptation. The spirit truly is ready, but the flesh is weak." And again he went away, and prayed, and spake the same words. And when again he returned he found them asleep again (for their eyes were heavy), neither wist they what to answer him. And he cometh the third time, and saith unto them, "Sleep on now, and take your rest: it is enough, the hour is come; behold, the Son of man is betrayed into the hands of sinners. Rise up, let us go; he that betrayeth me is at hand."

And immediately, while he yet spake, cometh Judas, one of the twelve, and with him a great multitude with swords and staves, from the chief priests and the scribes and the elders. And he that betrayed him had given them a token, saying, "Whomsoever I shall kiss, that same is he; take him, and lead him away safely." And as soon as he was come, he goeth straightway to him, and saith, "Master, master," and kissed him.

And they laid their hands on him, and took him.

And one of them that stood by drew a sword, and smote a servant of the high priest, and cut off his ear. And Jesus answered and said unto them, "Are ye come out, as against a thief, with swords and with staves to take me? I was daily with you in the temple teaching, and ye took me not: but the scriptures must be fulfilled." And they all forsook him, and fled.

And there followed him a certain young man, having a linen cloth cast about his naked body; and the young men laid hold on him; and he left the linen cloth, and fled from them naked. And they led Jesus away to the high priest: and with him were assembled the chief priests and the elders and the scribes.

MARK 14:32–53

§

And they said, "Lord, behold, here are two swords." And he said unto them, "It is enough." And he came out, and went, as he was wont, to the mount of Olives, and his disciples also followed him. And when he was at the place, he said unto them, "Pray that ye enter not into temptation." And he was withdrawn from them about a stone's cast, and kneeled down, and prayed, saying, "Father, if thou be willing, remove this cup from me: nevertheless not my will, but thine, be done." And there appeared an angel unto him from heaven, strengthening him. And being in an agony he prayed more earnestly: and his sweat was as it were great drops of blood falling down to the ground.

And when he rose up from prayer, and was come to his disciples, he found them sleeping for sorrow, and said unto them, "Why sleep ye? Rise and pray, lest ye enter into temptation." And while he yet spake, behold a multitude, and he that was called Judas, one of the twelve, went before them, and drew near unto Jesus to kiss him. But Jesus said unto him, "Judas, betrayest thou the Son of man with a kiss?" When they which were about him saw what would follow, they said unto him, "Lord shall we smite with the sword?" And one of them smote the servant of the high priest, and cut off his right ear. And Jesus answered and said, "Suffer ye thus far." And he touched his ear, and healed him.

Then Jesus said unto the chief priests and the captains of the temple, and the elders, which were come to him, "Be ye come out, as against a thief, with swords and staves? When I was daily with you in the temple, ye stretched forth no hands against me: but this is your hour, and the power of darkness." Then they took him, and led him, and brought him into the high priest's house.

LUKE 22:38–54

❧

He went forth with his disciples over the brook Cedron, where was a garden, into the which he entered, and his disciples. And Judas also, which betrayed him, knew the place: for Jesus ofttimes resorted thither with his disciples. Judas then, having received a band of men and officers from the chief priests and Pharisees, cometh thither with lanterns and torches and weapons. Jesus therefore, knowing all things that should come upon him, went forth, and said unto them, "Whom seek ye?" They answered him, "Jesus of Nazareth." Jesus saith unto them, "I am he." And Judas also, which betrayed him, stood with them. As soon then as he had said unto them, "I am he," they went backward, and fell to the ground.

Then asked he them again, "Whom seek ye?" and they said, "Jesus of Nazareth."

Jesus answered, "I have told you that I am he: if therefore ye seek me, let these go their way." That the saying might be fulfilled which he spake, "Of them which thou gavest me have I lost none." Then Simon Peter having a sword drew it, and smote the high priest's servant, and cut off his right ear. The servant's name was Malchus.

Then said Jesus unto Peter, "Put up thy sword into the sheath: the cup which my Father hath given me, shall I not drink it?" Then the band and the captain and officers of the Jews took Jesus and bound him, and led him away to Annas first; for he was father-in-law to Caiaphas, which was the high priest that same year. JOHN 18:1–13

IT IS A SCENE played out in darkness.

Of the different darknesses that surround the story in my mind, one is domestic, personal. The darkness of my grandmother's bedroom.

My mother came from a family of nine: nine children all born alive and healthy from the womb of their large, austere, implacable mother. In my generation, there were twenty-one cousins. We all lived near my grandmother. We would often gather at her house for heavy, noisy, complicated meals. Usually supper: pasta, called spaghetti, with meatballs and tomato sauce, perhaps lasagna, then a ham, then custard and a cake made with raisins or dried fruits.

When the raucous and contentious meal was over, and the grown-ups moved into the living room to do whatever it was they did there, we children were set free to roam the house. Wherever we began, we always ended in the same place as if to quieten ourselves, to sober ourselves from the large drunkenness of family life. We were frightened of our grandmother's bedroom, of its darkness, the secrets we knew were there but did not know how to locate or even to name. Timidly, as if we knew that we were stealing grace, we would click on the metal light that was clipped to the metal sideboard of our grandmother's bed. And when the insufficient light was struck, our eye fell always on the object of our great fascination: a picture made of slats, a picture that become two pictures if you turned your head. One way, you saw a pastel Sacred Heart, Jesus pointing to something in the middle of his chest the shape of a pimento, or a tongue, or flame. But if you tilted your head the other way, you saw a picture made of dark tones of blue and blue-black: the only light spot faced Jesus as he knelt, praying.

The Agony in the Garden. I can recall no time in my life when those words were not mine. As close, as personal as my birth date or my address.

But what could a child have understood of the word "agony"? I understood that it was something about darkness, of the fear of darkness, the same fear that caused me to insist upon a night-light long after I was too old to warrant such indulgence. To imagine that children, even fortunate, protected children, are innocent of dread is to subscribe to a delusion. Certainly, I knew dread. I experienced it every Sunday night, in the blank space before sleep when contemplating the beginning of a new school week. But I didn't connect my personal dread with Jesus, kneeling in the darkness. Jesus was God. I could not put myself in his place, the place of the picture made of plastic slats.

And so, the word "agony," by its very domestication, having been transformed into cheap, mass-produced artifacts like my grand-mother's picture, has had its gravity stolen. The word has taken on the tincture of exaggeration or of melodrama. We can imagine the jilted lover in a silent movie, ringleted, mouthing, "Oh, Agony," reproduced in white letters on a dark background just before the stock brilliantined villain carries off the beloved.

So I would prefer to think of the scene as "The Dread in the Dark Garden." One of the difficulties of talking about it is determining what it is, then deciding where the scene begins. The difficulty is exacerbated because the scene in the garden flows so seamlessly from the events of the Last Supper, particularly the moment in which Jesus hands Judas the bread dipped in wine and names him the betrayer. Why not then begin with the sentence in John, which tells that Judas left the room and goes on to say, "And it was night"? This has an undeniable appeal: the austerity of a sentence that is pure spondee, a sentence so simple that no simpler could be imagined.

But John makes no mention of what has come to be known as "the Agony in the Garden." In his Gospel, there is no vision of Jesus praying in dread. What is recorded is only his entrapment, his capture, the betrayal of Judas, the cutting off of the servant's ear. John, the most mystical, the most intellectual, the most metaphysical of the Evangelists, doesn't make a place for the sufferer of mental anguish. And this omission blocks the point of entry for those who have suffered in this way.

Because this scene is so psychological and so narratively dramatic, I attended with special care to the different translations that describe Jesus' mental state. I examined different translations—the New Revised Standard, the King James, the Oxford, and the Douay-Rheims—to see how these mental states were described. It is a commonplace among literary types that the King James version, in providing the most beautiful English, also provides the most satisfactory reading experience. I have not always found it to be the case, but this scene, with its somber overtones, seems particularly appropriate to the diction of the Jacobean age (we forget that the source of "Jacobean" is the same James who gave his name to this translation), and so seems most congenial to that translation. It was, after all, an age that specialized in the complexity of doom.

The New Revised Standard translation describes Matthew's Jesus as "grieved and agitated," Mark's as "distressed and agitated," "deeply grieved, even to death," Luke's as in "anguish." The Oxford renders the same states as "distress and anguish overwhelmed him" in Matthew; "horror and anguish overwhelmed him" and "My heart is ready to break with grief" in Mark; and in Luke as "in an anguish of spirit." The King James says Jesus is "sorrowful and very heavy" in Matthew; "sore amazed and very heavy," his soul "exceedingly sorrowful unto death" in Mark; and "in an agony" in Luke's version. The Douay-Rheims says that in Matthew, "he began to grow sorrowful and to be sad," in Mark (where the garden of Gethsemene is referred to as a "farm"), "he began to fear and to be heavy," and his soul as "sorrowful even unto death." In Luke, he is described identically to the King James as "being in an agony."

What happens, exactly, in this scene? Jesus brings his disciples to the garden. He retreats from them and prays. In Matthew and Mark, his anguish makes him restless. Rhythmically, there are jarring alterations between movement and stasis, inquiry and rest. He doesn't know whether to throw himself into solitary prayer, to abandon himself entirely to a position that he knows is hopeless, useless, an empty request, and to stay in this relationship with his father, or to return to his disciples for companionship. In both Matthew and Mark, Jesus moves from willed separation to eager attempts at connection with his disciples six times: three times he leaves the disciples and three times he comes back. Three times he finds them sleeping, each time pathetically hoping against hope that it will be different. The betrayal of their absence from him in sleep foreshadows the betrayal of Judas that will follow soon after. Only Luke, of the four Evangelists the most tenderhearted (though inconsistently so), understands that they may be "sleeping for sorrow."

But Luke's tenderness of heart makes his portrayal of this scene most vulnerable to sentimentality. When Jesus is praying alone, Luke includes a description of drops of sweat that fall to the ground like drops of blood: it is to him we owe the cliché "sweating blood." And in Luke's garden, there is a comforting angel. The picture in my grandmother's bedroom was all Luke's fault.

Matthew and Mark do nothing to alleviate Jesus' sense of bereftness, sorrow unaccompanied and unalloyed. In Luke's rendering, Jesus does not keep going back and forth from the disciples to solitary prayer. And so it lacks the sense of increasing tension that Matthew's and Mark's versions provide.

After Jesus declares to his disciples that the time is come for him to be delivered to the enemies, Judas arrives, accompanied by the cohort of the High Priest. The somber silence of the night is broken. Whereas Jesus prayed silently and his disciples slept, now there is the hubbub of accusation. I always saw torches lighting this part of the scene; I was surprised that in all the rendering of the betrayal and capture (John weighs in at this point), there is not a syllable about torchlight.

The Judas kiss is given: a quick betrayal, over almost before it is begun. Then the disciples panic. One of them—John—names Peter as the one who cuts off the ear of the servant of the High Priest. Was this done by one of the two swords referred to in Luke when the apostle says, "Here are two swords," and Jesus replies, "It is enough"? Does he mean "enough" as in, "Two is fine, we don't need three," or does he mean enough as in, "Enough already"? Was it another example of the apostles' propensity for miscomprehension, or did Jesus change his mind in the garden when he touched the servant's ear (this occurs only in Luke) and replaced it, saying, "He that lives by the sword will perish by the sword"?

At this point in Mark's version, a very strange incident occurs. A young man wrapped in a linen cloth is caught hold of, but he drops the linen cloth and runs naked into the darkness. Nothing leads up to it and nothing leads away from it. Nothing explains it. It is pure visual image: shimmering in the darkness, unattached. A hint of homoerotic sexuality; a flash in the dark night.

Jesus is taken away. The final act of the tragedy of his death is set in motion.

. . .

I IMAGINE IT AS A NIGHT without a moon. I see the dark wood of the olive trees: I have been to Gethsemene and the trees there have nothing of the silver darkness of their Italian cousins. What light there was cast rocks into menacing shadows: undifferentiated, nothing creates the distinctness that is a bulwark against dread. Everything natural was transformed to portent. The landscape of the soul's dark night.

The episode could be read as a poem that explores the tones of darkness. It is important to remember that darkness is not one thing. There are many tones *of* darkness. There are many tones *to* darkness. What do we find if we make a list of all these descriptions, as if we were making of it a found poem?

Grieved and agitated
Sorrowful and very heavy
Distress and anguish overwhelmed him
He began to grow sorrowful and to be sad

Distressed and agitated
Sore amazed and very heavy
Horror and anguish overwhelmed him
He began to fear and be heavy

My soul is exceedingly sorrowful unto death
I am deeply grieved, even to death
My heart is ready to break with grief
My soul is sorrowful even unto death

In agony
In anguish of spirit
In his anguish.

This scene in the dark garden is, of all the scenes in the Gospel, the most difficult to reconcile with the idea of Jesus as omnipotent, omniscient God. How can God dread? Dread, the horror of the future, which seems inevitable, mixed with the desire to be spared. But if Jesus was God, wouldn't he have known from all eternity that he would come to earth to die? How can our minds adapt to the idea of divine hesitation, divine reluctance? A god like us, not as we wish we were but as we hope never to be?

It raises the question: Why do we require a man-God? Is it to give us, in our despair of our own aloneness, a sense of accompaniment, a conviction that we are connected to the source and center of all life, connected by a person with a face that we can comprehend as registering emotions something like our own? At once beyond time and on our side. What does it mean if we must call this person God?

The dreading god
Supplicating and refused
Heartbroken
Grieved and agitated
Sorrowful and sad
Heavy
Overwhelmed.

THE IMPULSE TO BEND THE KNEE to such a god might feel less like capitulation to a tyrant than an acknowledgment of our grievous and grief-stricken lot.

7

The Fig
Tree

In the morning, when he returned to the city, he was hungry. And seeing a fig tree by the side of the road, he went to it and found nothing at all on it but leaves. Then he said to it, "May no fruit ever come from you again!" And the fig tree withered at once. When the disciples saw it, they were amazed, saying, "How did the fig tree wither at once?" Jesus answered them, "Truly I tell you, if you have faith and do not doubt, not only will you do what has been done to the fig tree, but even if you say to this mountain, 'Be lifted up and thrown into the sea,' it will be done. Whatever you ask for in prayer with faith, you will receive."

MATTHEW 21:18–22

❧

On the following day, when they came from Bethany, he was hungry. Seeing in the distance a fig tree in leaf, he went to see whether perhaps he would find anything on it. When he came to it, he found nothing but leaves, for it was not the season for figs. He said to it, "May no one ever eat fruit from you again." And his disciples heard it. . . . In the morning as they passed by, they saw the fig tree withered away to its roots. Then Peter remembered and said to him, "Rabbi, look! The fig tree that you cursed has withered." Jesus answered them, "Have faith in God. Truly I tell you, if you say to this mountain, 'Be taken up and thrown into the sea,' and if you do not doubt in your heart, but believe that what you say will come to pass, so it will be done for you. So I tell you, whatever you ask for in prayer, believe that you have received it, and it will be yours. Whenever you stand praying, forgive, if you have anything against anyone; so that your Father in heaven may also forgive your trespasses.

MARK 11:12–14, 20–25

THIS IS NOT A SCENE that was important to me in my childhood. I try to understand why some Gospel passages are resonant for me and some are not. Why, for example, does my mind skate over the parable of the Good Samaritan and the image of the Good Shepherd? Is it that, even as a child, I was on the alert against cliché, determined to assert my differentness, my imaginative individuality, my separation from the common lot? And then, of course, there is the accident of association. I had never seen a fig tree; I had never eaten a fresh fig. When I heard "fig," I immediately thought of "Fig Newton," a cookie I deeply disliked, a sticky seedy filling surrounded by a soft substance, neither cookie nor biscuit, dissatisfying, dull, unfresh.

But to come upon this story in adulthood is to be disturbed and shocked. It is distressing, and it has the thrill of all unnatural acts. It complicates the pastel portrait of gentle Jesus meek and mild, overpainting it with a Mannerist palette: acid green, irritable rose pink, an under hint of a metallic, cobalt blue. Bitter to the tongue. The taste of Campari, of arugula. Spite, pique, petulance, caprice. We could imagine this kind of behavior from Zeus, or Hera—but of the God of Love? The author of the Beatitudes? Even Yahweh, with all his ups and downs, would be incapable of a punishment called down by no ethical transgression, no idolatry, no breach of covenant, but simply because one is doing what one is meant to be doing at the appointed time.

As a moment, it is at once comic and terrible. The powerful man, hungry, using his power like a frustrated child. Jesus, the child tyrant. Jesus, the bully of the world. Jesus, the failure.

We love it because it is us. We are disappointed, because he is no better than we are at our most irrational, when we are being our least admirable selves. Shaking our fists at a rain-filled sky. Kicking at the door of a closed restaurant, because the restaurateur is pointing at his watch, indicting the propriety of his decision to remain closed.

It enacts our helpless rage at the grip of the null. Our impotence before the way things are. Our fury at the prospect of the limits, the failures of our creativity, the resistance to the imagination. Only in the imagination could figs ripen out of season. Just try it, Jesus says to the fig tree, and the fig tree refuses, stuck in the paralysis of the habitual. Jesus cursing the fig tree is an image of us banging our heads against the limits of our own creativity: our inability to make ourselves bear fruit. Fruit out of season. Brought to life by our will.

What a powerful word is the word "wither." We feel it in our blood and lymph-bearing organs, all the vessels of the body that are conduits of fluid life. Withering: the instant drying up of life. Of the life force. Finished for good. At a word.

We read this episode with a kind of sadomasochistic thrill at the reversal of the laws of nature.

At a word.

JESUS CURSES THE FIG TREE when he seems to be riding the wave of power. In both Matthew and Mark, this act follows the triumphal procession into Jerusalem; in Matthew, Jesus curses the fig tree immediately after he banishes the moneylenders from the temple; in Mark, the incident of the fig tree is sandwiched between the two more dramatic events. Is the resistance of the fig tree a sign from the father that Jesus needs to understand the limits of his power: that he is not above the laws of Nature, which are the laws of God? Later on, both Matthew and Mark, as if abashed by the Master's bad behavior, have him put the incident in the context of faith. In Matthew, the disciples ask, "How did the fig tree wither at once?" Jesus answers them, "Truly I tell you, if you have faith and do not doubt, not only will you do what has been done to the fig tree, but even if you say to this mountain, 'Be lifted up and thrown into the sea,' it will be done. Whatever you ask for in prayer with faith, you will receive." And here is Mark: "In the morning as they passed by, they saw the fig tree withered away to its roots. Then Peter remembered and said to him, 'Rabbi look! The fig tree that you cursed has withered.' Jesus answered them, 'Have faith in God. Truly I tell you, if you say to this mountain, "Be taken up and thrown into the sea," and if you do not doubt in your heart, but believe that what you say will come to pass, it will be done for you. So I tell you, whatever you ask for in prayer, believe that you have received it, and it will be yours.'"

Perhaps this is the most distressing aspect of the story: that the power of faith can be used for destruction as well as healing. Jesus is able to wither the tree, but not to make it bear fruit. So if it is meant to be a lesson on the power of faith the question arises: what was the point, the fruit or the withering? The straight line of ethical quid pro quo is broken: it is not as easy as we would like. Power is what we are dealing with, and power is not always benign. We might wish that Jesus were more like Santa Claus, more Candide than Christ. But he is who he is . . . a man of passion, sometimes overtaken by himself.

And what is the nature of the curse? Not to be eaten from. Not to be consumed. Not to be of use. Not to be able to do what one is made for. "May you never bear fruit." The curse of sterility. No more life. Have we not, all of us, felt the curse, "No more life for you. Never again"? A curse particularly feared by the naturally fecund. The terrifying question we fear having to ask ourselves one day: how then will I live out the rest of my natural life? Withered. Dried up. Cursed.

Accursed. Simone Weil said, "I never read the story of the barren fig tree without trembling. I think that it is a portrait of me."*

There is an interesting sentence at the end of the scene in Mark. After reporting Jesus' curse, "May no one ever eat from you again," Mark notes, "And his disciples heard it." A thought naturally arises: perhaps he wished or meant not to be heard?

THE NEXT WORDS OUT OF JESUS' MOUTH are an exhortation to forgiveness. But what of the fig tree? It has not received forgiveness. It is withered. Dead for good. As far as we can see, the withering has won.

Reading the story as I do, I encounter a Jesus who is far from perfect. I wondered how this might be experienced by readers who, unlike me, have a stake in a Jesus without contradictions and without flaws. I read many commentaries, from St. Augustine to contemporary theologians, to devout bloggers, to hyper-literalists who insist that though you wouldn't think it, the early leaves on the tree indicate that there actually is fruit that Jesus sees. I even find one enraged Web site whose motto is "The Church of Theists Suck." What I discover in all these commentators is a tendency to hop right over the presentness of the narrative moment—with its inclusion of contradiction and complexity, and its focus on the personality of the leading character—to a simplified metaphoric and symbolic interpretation. For these commentators, the fig tree is the Jewish people, and the curse is a punishment for their failure of belief in Jesus. Often, they seem determined to hurtle toward the "faith can move mountains"

---

* Simone Weil, *Waiting for God*, (New York and San Francisco: Harper Colophon, 1973), p. 100.

section, a more comfortable place to stand than the one that tries to explain Jesus cursing a tree for doing what it was meant to. But in the encounter with the fig tree, faith does not triumph, even the faith of the man-God. Unless you define faith as the power to destroy. Jesus' gesture is useless: he does not get what he wants. The tree will not bear fruit and he will not be fed. He is playing the zero-sum game of vengeance versus the intractable. The mountain can be cast into the sea, but figs will not grow out of season.

When we see Jesus cursing the fig tree, we observe him partaking of our despair over the death grip, the death sentence of causality. We must apprehend him here as a figure outside, past, the lines of good behavior. It is a narrative unfolding of what I believe to be one of the most important Gospel truths: that not everything turns out well.

8

The Temptation
in the Desert

Then Jesus was led up by the Spirit into the wilderness to be tempted by the devil. He fasted forty days and forty nights, and afterwards he was famished. The tempter came and said to him, "If you are the Son of God, command these stones to become loaves of bread." But he answered, "It is written, 'One does not live by bread alone, but by every word that comes from the mouth of God.'"

Then the devil took him to the holy city and placed him on the pinnacles of the temple, saying to him, "If you are the Son of God, throw yourself down; for it is written, 'He will command his angels concerning you,' and 'On their hands they will bear you up, so that you will not dash your foot against a stone.'"

Jesus said to him, "Again it is written, 'Do not put the Lord your God to the test.'"

Again, the devil took him to a very high mountain and showed him all the kingdoms of the world and their splendor; and he said to him, "All these I will give you, if you will fall down and worship me." Jesus said to him, "Away with you, Satan! for it is written, 'Worship the Lord your God, and serve only him.'"

Then the devil left him, and suddenly angels came and waited on him. MATTHEW 4:1–11

§

Jesus, full of the Holy Spirit, returned from the Jordan and was led by the Spirit in the wilderness, where for forty days he was tempted by the devil. He ate nothing at all during those days, and when they were over, he was famished. The devil said to him, "If you are the Son of God, command this stone to become a loaf of bread." Jesus answered him, "It is written, 'One does not live by bread alone.'"

Then the devil led him up and showed him in an instant all the kingdoms of the world. And the devil said to him, "To you I will give their glory and all this authority; for it has been given over to me, and I give it to anyone I please. If you, then, will worship me, it will all be yours." Jesus answered him, "It is written, 'Worship the Lord your God, and serve only him.'"

Then the devil took him to Jerusalem, and placed him on the pinnacle of the temple, saying to him, "If you are the Son of God, throw yourself down from here, for it is written, 'He will command his angels concerning you, to protect you,' and 'On their hands they will bear you up, so that you will not dash your foot against a stone.'" Jesus answered him, "It is said, 'Do not put the Lord your God to the test.'" LUKE 4:1–12

THE INCIDENT OF THE TEMPTATION in the Desert is elaborated in Matthew and Luke, and mentioned briefly in Mark. But how did they know about it? Presumably, Jesus was alone in the desert with Satan. Except for the Agony in the Garden, this is the only time in which the writers report on something that happened when no one was around to hear it. And so, formal questions arise, questions of literary strategy. How is Jesus known? And by whom? How do the tellers know what it is they say they know?

All three Evangelists include the Temptation immediately after Jesus' baptism by John, and the voice from the heaven naming him the beloved son. In Luke, the first words we hear Jesus speaking are spoken to the devil. His first words: a refusal. He will not turn stone to bread. Man does not live by bread alone. In Matthew, this is Jesus' second sentence. His first is likewise a refusal: of John's assertion that Jesus should baptize him, a demurral, an assertion of modesty, an unwillingness to place himself at the top. These words, "Let it be so now; for it is proper for us in this way to fulfill all righteousness" (Matthew 3:15), are spoken by Jesus as the disciple of John, in tradition his slightly older cousin, probably a radical ascetic with whom Jesus studied before he moved on. So his later rejoinder to Satan, "Man does not live by bread alone," can be understood, in both Matthew and Luke, to be Jesus' first sentence upon understanding his mission. His first way of expressing who he is, by asserting who he is not, what he will not do: turn stone into bread, throw himself from the pinnacle, bow down before Satan so that he may have earthly power.

Jesus' refusal indicates his understanding that this is neither the time nor the place for such an action. He has withdrawn into the desert for a period of self-discovery, of contemplation rather than action. He will not cut short his time to silence the voice of self-doubt. Prove it, the tempter says. No need, Jesus replies.

One of the rare human achievements is to be so sure of oneself that one resists the temptation to prove one's own worth to someone else. Think of the extraordinary strength to resist what is offered by the voice in the wilderness: prove you are effective, prove you are beloved, try authority on for size, and on top of it, glory. Prove you can be obeyed and praised. Prove you have it in you to rule the world.

To reach maturity in life and work, these are the temptations that must be resisted. To resist them is to say, "I know who I am and my actions—which I have not yet started to perform—will make that clear." For an artist, Jesus' refusal of the temptation to turn stone to bread represents the refusal of the crowd-pleasing trick. I am reminded of the lines from Auden's "In Praise of Limestone": "to . . . ruin a fine tenor voice / For effects that bring down the house, could happen to all / But the best and the worst of us."

At first, it is distressing to hear Jesus refusing to turn stone to bread. Is he disregarding the anguish of the hungry in order to make an abstract point . . . about the nature of his ministry, about his place in relation to the tempter? But there are no hungry present, and so Jesus would be turning stone to bread for the "effect" that could "bring down the house," his father's house, the house of the Kingdom of God which he is preparing for those who will enter. Jesus is alone in the desert, except for the tempter. Carried back to the hungry on the plain or at the shore, the bread would be retransformed to stone. So the miracle would not be a radical act that assuaged human suffering, it would be a performance piece.

The second temptation is put in terms of filial relationship. It begins, "If you are the son of God . . . ," then your father will send angels to save you. It raises the question of a belief in one's own lovability, in one's own having been loved. And who of us is so sure of a father's love, and so free of need to demonstrate it to a hostile other, that he wouldn't try out the paternal assertion "I will send my angels. Nothing can happen to you"? Which of us wouldn't be tempted to say, "You want to see how much my father loves me? I'll show you right now." The miracle of the resistance of this temptation, of the three the most poignant because it is the most accessible, is precisely the miraculous spectacle of one so entirely secure in love that he can silence the mocking onlooker. So unshakable in his conviction that he can say to the dark voice: "You are of no interest to me, no importance. Go away."

And which of us would have the strength to resist authority, glory? To be deferred to, to be admired. Obeyed. To have dominion. "Look out over the whole world. See what you see. All of it is yours."

Authority. Glory. What are they but the signs that the world recognizes our worth? What Jesus is really resisting in Satan's temptations is the need for recognition. He will do what he must do because he is meant to do it. The pure act without residue of anxiety, uncertainty, or fear. From the outset, Jesus understands how the appetite for recognition must inevitably corrupt. Why else would he keep telling the people he cured to keep it to themselves?

His tone is quiet, almost playful, as if he were engaging Satan in a game of tennis, or chess. There is none of the outraged anger he will later direct at the Pharisees. Formally, it has many elements in common with heroic contests . . . with the playful elements of warlike games.

MANY VISUAL ARTISTS, writers, and thinkers, from Duccio and Dürer and Thomas Cole to Pasolini and Andrew Lloyd Weber, have used the Temptation in the Desert as the foundation for their own work. The most famous use of this episode is found in the Grand Inquisitor parable of Dostoyevsky's *The Brothers Karamazov.*

Thou didst promise them the bread of Heaven, but, I repeat again, can it compare with earthly bread in the eyes of the weak, ever sinful and ignoble race of man? And if for the sake of the bread of Heaven thousands and tens of thousands shall follow Thee, what is to become of the millions and tens of thousands of millions of creatures who will not have the strength to forego the earthly bread for the sake of the heavenly? Or dost Thou care only for the tens of thousands of the great and strong, while the millions, numerous as the sands of the sea, who are weak but love Thee, must exist only for the sake of the great and strong?

... Yet what was offered Thee? There are three powers, three powers alone, able to conquer and to hold captive forever the conscience of these impotent rebels for their happiness— those forces are miracle, mystery and authority. Thou hast rejected all three and hast set the example for doing so. When the wise and dread spirit set Thee on the pinnacle of the temple and said to Thee, "If Thou wouldst know whether Thou art the Son of God then cast Thyself down, for it is written: the angels shall hold him up lest he fall and bruise himself, and Thou shalt know then whether Thou art the Son of God and shalt prove then how great is Thy faith in Thy Father." But Thou didst refuse and wouldst not cast Thyself down.... Hadst Thou taken the world and Caesar's purple, Thou wouldst have founded the universal state and have given universal peace.

The parable occurs in the context of a conversation between Ivan, the cynical, freethinking brother, and Alyosha, the believing seminarian brother. Ivan has been tormenting Alyosha with tales of cruelty to children, suggesting that the suffering of children is a proof against the existence of a loving God. Having done this, he invents a tale of the return of Jesus to a Spain torn apart by the Inquisition.

Jesus is captured and taken prisoner, and questioned by the Grand Inquisitor, a man grown old in the service of his ideal. The Inquisitor accuses Jesus of creating an impossible situation for humans by refusing "miracle, mystery and authority"—the analogues to the three temptations: to turn stone to bread, to throw himself from the pinnacle, to assume earthly power. He chides Jesus for having resisted Satan's temptations on the grounds that to have given in to them would have been to have demanded fealty from human beings, rather than waiting for their free approach, an approach motivated by love. The Inquisitor says that Jesus has made things too hard for human beings in allowing them their freedom, and that the Inquisitor and his kind, in understanding human weakness, are the ones who really love them. He is prepared to burn Jesus in an auto-da-fé, but at the last minute inexplicably lets him go. And Jesus, who has been silent during the entire encounter, leaves in silence, with a kiss. Like Judas.

Dostoyevsky uses the temptations as a sign of the conflict between the idea of a loving God and the reality of human suffering, of the challenge which he believes is the genius of Christianity: the demand to love freely rather than to submit through fear and compulsion. The always ironical Ivan offers no solution or resolution, and his stance is deeply painful to his loving brother.

Deeply distressed by the story, Alyosha asks his brother, "How will you live, how will you love?" For Alyosha, the meaning of life, the ability to love, are based on an image of God embodied in the figure of Jesus. And, in fact, Ivan's fate is to live in madness, unable to love. Yet Alyosha's alternative, to live for "the little sticky leaves, the precious tombs, the blue skies, the woman you love," seems far too weak to confront the reality of abused and suffering children.

AMONG THE CONTEMPORARY INTERPRETERS of this Gospel episode is the current Pope; he explores it in a book on Jesus written while he was still known as Joseph Ratzinger. Pondering the first temptation, Benedict/Ratzinger speaks to the problem of Jesus' refusal to turn stone to bread, suggesting as it does a failure of empathy for the hungry who could be eating it. "Is there anything more tragic, is there anything more opposed to belief in the existence of a good God and a Redeemer of mankind, than world hunger? Shouldn't it be the first test of the Redeemer, before the world's gaze and on the world's behalf, to give it bread and end all hunger?"

He goes on to note that God fed the people of Israel in the desert, and poses the question: "Isn't the problem of feeding the world—and, more generally, are not social problems—the primary, true yardstick by which redemption has to be measured? ... Marxism—quite understandably—made this very point the core of its promise of salvation."* By including in the same sentence the words "Marxism" and "salvation," Benedict, the sworn enemy of Marxism, is using an old debator's trick: pretend to grant your enemy the ground on which he stands before you cut it out from under him.

---

* Joseph Ratzinger, Pope Benedict XVI, *Jesus of Nazareth*, (New York: Doubleday, 2007), pp. 31–33.

And, using another strategy, he adopts for a moment the tone of the skeptical interlocutor taking up the question of the Church's responsibility for feeding the hungry: "If you claim to be the Church of God, then start by making sure the world has bread—the rest comes later." Appearing to take the challenge seriously, he responds, "It is hard to answer this challenge, precisely because the cry of the hungry penetrates so deeply into the ears and into the soul—as well it should."

It penetrates, yes ("as well it should"!), but not to the greatest depths. Ratzinger puts the stone/bread temptation in the context of other bread narratives, beginning with the multiplication of the loaves and fishes, the episode when Jesus takes five loaves and three fishes and turns them into enough food for five thousand who had come to hear him preach. Why, he asks, did Jesus then perform a miracle with bread when earlier he rejected it? One might think that it's because, in the desert, the offer was made by Satan, and on the plain, it was the spectacle of human hunger that moved Jesus. But not at all. The reason, according to Ratzinger, that Jesus multiplied the loaves and fishes was not just to feed the hungry because they were hungry, but that they deserved to be fed since they had listened. This miracle, he says, was "preceded by the search for God, for his word, for the teaching that sets the whole of life on the right path. . . . Jesus is not indifferent toward men's hunger, their bodily needs, but he places these things in the proper context and the proper order." He quotes a German Jesuit, Alfred Delp, who was executed by the Nazis: "Bread is important, freedom is more important, but most important of all is unbroken fidelity and faithful adoration."

Dostoyevsky ends in anguished uncertainty; Ratzinger ends with a secure hierarchy: faithful adoration, freedom, bread. What would Ivan Karamazov say to that?

Dostoyevsky and Ratzinger both use the Temptation story to make a point about the right ordering of the world. Dostoyevsky, a citizen of the nineteenth century, focuses on the implications of this scene for an understanding of human freedom. (It also allows him a slap in the face to the Roman Church, which was always Orthodox Fyodor's idea of a good time.) Pope Benedict uses the Temptation to remind us, most importantly, that "man does not live by bread alone," and that concern for human hunger must be contextualized and put in its proper place, the body's place, a place far below the exalted altitudes of "unbroken fidelity" and "faithful adoration." An altitude that is most comfortable to the kind of Catholic he prefers—the kind that doesn't ask those pesky questions about obedience and authority.

Of course, I, too, make my own use of the Temptation in the Desert. It compels me as a moment in which we glimpse Jesus in the process of the creation of a self. A self created by a radical withdrawal. Not only from people and the comforts of civilization, but a withdrawal into a featureless landscape, a landscape devoid of distraction, distinction. Literally devoid of nourishment.

On this reading, I am particularly taken by the word "famished." Matthew and Luke both use it in the newer translations. In the King James the word is simply "hungered"; for once, the new is poetically more resonant than the old. Famished: you can feel it in the cave behind your ribs, in the midriff's empty drum. Famished: it suggests depletion, an almost dangerous, desperate state. Jesus was famished. Vulnerable.

Suppose we understand the temptations as a vision induced by starvation in the desert—Luke says the devil went on tempting him for forty days. Forty days without food, forty days of psychological torment. Suppose we think of Satan as a product of Jesus' own mind, the great mind that understood what the things were that could really get in the way of the importance of his work. I can understand the accusation leveled against such an interpretation: that I am flattening the shining metaphysical mountain into a pancake of the psychological in my quest to make it my own. But to my mind, if the temptations are products of the mind of Jesus, they are all the more precious. Because what is eternal about their rightness, and recognizable in their rightness to most thoughtful humans, whatever they think of Jesus, is not the personification of evil in the form of a fallen angel, but the precise evocation of the particular flavors of darkness represented by the three tests.

The tests Jesus needs to pass before he can assume authority on his own terms, or his father's. The temptations he must banish before he can reach full understanding of who he is.

Dostoyevsky's Inquisitor says:

The statement of those three questions was itself the miracle. If it were possible to imagine simply for the sake of argument that those three questions of the dread spirit had perished utterly from the books, and that we had to restore them and to invent them anew, and to do so had gathered together all the wise men of the earth—rulers, chief priests, learned men, philosophers, poets—and had set them the task to invent three questions, such as would not only fit the occasion, but express in three words, three human phrases, the whole future history of the world and of humanity—dost Thou believe that all the wisdom of the earth united could have invented anything in depth and force equal to the three questions which were actually put to Thee then by the wise and mighty spirit in the wilderness? . . .

As postmoderns, we are uneasy with the concept of miracle, and with the idea that any three questions could unite all the unsolved historical contradictions of human nature, or have connection to the eternal and the absolute. But if we examine the nature of the miracle the Inquisitor describes, we see that it is, in fact, a miracle in the form of questions, a miracle of language. A self-creating no.

9

The Writing
on the
Ground

And the scribes and Pharisees brought unto him a woman taken in adultery; and when they had set her in the midst, they say unto him, "Master, this woman was taken in adultery, in the very act. Now Moses in the law commanded us, that such should be stoned: but what sayest thou?" This they said, tempting him, that they might have to accuse him. But Jesus stooped down, and with his finger wrote on the ground, as though he heard them not. So when they continued asking him, he lifted up himself, and said unto them, "He that is without sin among you, let him first cast a stone at her." And again he stooped down, and wrote on the ground. And they which heard it, being convicted by their own conscience, went out one by one, beginning at the eldest, even unto the last: and Jesus was left alone, and the woman standing in the midst. When Jesus had lifted up himself, and saw none but the woman, he said unto her, "Woman, where are those thine accusers? hath no man condemned thee?" She said, "No man, Lord." And Jesus said unto her, "Neither do I condemn thee: go, and sin no more." JOHN 8:3–11

THIS IS ANOTHER SCENE I did not focus on in childhood. I think this is because it was always known as "The Woman Taken in Adultery," and the word "adultery" was one I had a hard time getting a grip on; it seemed to be, by its very name, something in the province of adults. Usually this would be a category I would be eager to explore, but the word "adultery" seemed to carry no glamour with it, only a defiling shame, and I had far enough of that in my own dark fears to want to approach it in the life of Jesus.

But coming to it as a woman with her own sexual past, as a feminist, and as a writer, I find it has become among the most precious Gospel moments to me, particularly precious because in it we see Jesus the writer (*pace* Raymond Brown). Making a mark. Making language in the dirt, with his own finger. He doesn't even use a stick. The words are made by his own body: flesh made word. The task of the rest of me and my kind. Writers.

It is, of course, also an image of illegibility.

THE SCENE OCCURS ONLY IN JOHN, and some commentators think it doesn't belong there, that it really belongs to Luke. Perhaps it is because it seems too rooted in the body and in ordinary event—so different from John's dominant tone: mystical, abstract, intellectual.

It begins early in the morning. Jesus is teaching in the temple; a crowd gathers to hear him. Suddenly, there is an interruption. The scribes and Pharisees bring him a woman who was taken in adultery.

The interruption is one of violence. It is a violent act to "take" someone in adultery. Before this scene, there must have been the scene we do not see: the shame of nakedness, of being caught out. Where is the man, the partner in crime? He is, of course, absent. Tactfully removed; graciously apart.

Did the scribes and Pharisees look upon her in her nakedness? Did she stand, naked, and then dress herself in front of them? Was the whole situation scopophilically arousing to them? There are echoes of the story of Susanna and the Elders from the Old Testament Book of Daniel. But the differences are important. In the older story, Daniel is defending an innocent woman, a chaste, falsely accused wife who is being blackmailed by lecherous old men who say they will make everyone believe she is meeting with a young lover if she refuses to have sex with them. Daniel tricks them in their lie, and they are put to death. But the woman in John's Gospel, unlike Susanna, nameless, is also, unlike Susanna, guilty of the transgression of which she has been accused. And unlike Susanna, her sexual allure is not part of the picture. So Jesus is not defending the desirable innocent, he is questioning the whole idea of guilt.

She does not deny the accusations; she is silent before those who accuse her. It is impossible to imagine her as anything but silent. Her silence is important to the dramatic balance of the scene, which traverses the territory between tumult and quiet, aggression and passivity, the power of righteousness and the impotence of transgression, accusation and forgiveness, contempt and respite.

The woman is a plaything, a pawn, a cipher, a counter in the game of entrapping Jesus. She is nothing to the men who accuse her. In the New English Bible, they make "her stand in front of them," in the King James and the Douay-Rheims, "they set her in the midst." The sullied women is placed (she does not place herself) in front of or in the midst of the unsullied men. Unflanked. Unprotected. Alone.

Then the accusation comes to the fore: "Master, this woman was taken in adultery. In the very act." In the different versions, "This woman was caught in the very act of committing adultery," "This woman was even now taken in adultery." And then, the invocation of the law, "Now in the law, Moses commanded us to stone such women. Now what do you say?" "Now Moses in the law commanded us that such should be stoned: but what sayest thou?" "Now Moses in the law commanded us to stone such a one. But what sayest thou?" Such women. Such. Such a one. She is turned into metonymy: a part for the whole. She stands for all women like herself, all adulterers, all sinners. Her name is "such." We hear the demand that as a "such" violence be perpetrated upon her, as a deterrent to her "suches," others of her kind. The loudness, the force of the accusation is followed by the invocation of a law.

What Jesus does next is a moment of greatness, both narratively and humanly. He doesn't answer the accusation. He says nothing. Of the human responses, silence in the face of an accusation is the most incomprehensible. How is an accuser, speaking in the name of law, and justice, to respond to silence? In fact, they do not respond. Their response, or lack of it, seems to be of no concern to Jesus.

He bends down. He writes something. Does anyone see what he writes? Who is it written for? Probably not for the Pharisees. The King James version, unlike more recent translations, includes the detail that Jesus writes "as though he had heard them not."

Or is he, like many writers, only writing to figure out what it is he really thinks?

If we were to see what the writing said, the moment would be more comprehensible, a useful moment, a moment that made a point. The point seems to be not to make a point.

What is created is an image of language-making that is devoid of content. The creation of an empty sign. In its emptiness, infinitely desirable.

And it raises the question, What is the relationship of writer to reader? What is writing if the reader is undefined? Isn't this the fate of all modern writers? We make marks, and we don't know for whom.

Does Jesus know? Does he write for the woman? Does he know whether or not the woman can read? It is likely that "such a woman" would not be literate. So what kind of writing is it?

But supposing what he wrote was a symbol or glyph, or a private language, legible only to her?

Suppose it is a charged moment of secret language, a private language, therefore all the world kept out, kept in silence, while the language is passed to only one? In Virginia Woolf's words, "A little language such as lovers use."

Whatever the nature of the language, Jesus and the woman partake in the relationship of writer to reader, a relationship that grows up in a pool of silence, a relationship of balance and imbalance: the reader is given words and gives back, what? Attention, interpretation.

Bursting out of silence, like a circus dog bursting through a paper hoop, Jesus responds to the accusation of the law, "Let anyone among you who is without sin be the first to throw a stone at her," or the cliché, "Let him who is without sin cast the first stone."

Now it is the Pharisees' turn to be silent. The accusers, buttressed by law. The accusers, using language in one of its loudest modes: accusation, the demand for a just punishment. Hearing the words of Jesus, they walk away wordless, the elders first. Only in the King James version is there a suggestion of moral consciousness on their parts; in this translation, they retreat "convicted by their own conscience."

In this moment an entire ethical system is born, and it is radical. It is not only that Jesus is undercutting the primacy of sexual sin committed by a woman. It is something much larger; it is, in fact, an upending of the very idea of an ethical system. What if judgment is impossible? It is, at first, an exhilarating thought; as we have all felt judged, all felt on the hook, we can all imagine the pleasure of being freed from the talons of judgment. A dizzying thought, but when considered, also sickening. As we are all sinners, we must understand that we are unfit to judge. If no judgment is possible, how do we live our lives? How do we counter evil? Or even name it? How do we know what's what? Where do we go from here? In this moment, Jesus demolishes the way that we know how to be. And offers in its place a private, illegible language, silence, the dispersal of the accusers and their law.

And he bends down and writes again. Something different? Or the same thing? The force of the repetition is invoked; he is not only writing, but rewriting. Is he revising?

The point is made that this writing, the act of writing, is central to the story, in a way that is not interpreted or made clear.

Jesus and the woman are left alone. "With the woman standing before him," "the woman standing in the midst." In the midst of what? Or is it simply the middle of the area where he had been teaching? Where he will continue to teach?

She has not moved. Jesus has bent down and got up twice. The others have moved away. She has only stood.

"Hath no man condemned thee?" It is a forceful word, "condemned," the same in all three translations. The verb "condemn" suggests a following prepositional phase: condemned to . . . to death? To eternal damnation? To a life as an outcast? It is stronger than accusation, stronger than punishment. Condemn—contemn—it suggests punishment but also a sense of hierarchy: I am better than you—how could you have done such a thing . . . I would never.

Finally, she speaks. She is asked, in effect, "Do you see, do you understand what has happened?" Her acknowledgment is demanded. She is not merely acted upon. "Has no man condemned you?" "No man, Lord." "Neither will I condemn you."

WHAT IS IT NOT TO BE CONDEMNED? To be not condemned?

I look the word up in *The Oxford English Dictionary* (the OED). Some definitions I find surprise me, some do not.

3. *esp.* with the penalty expressed, as *condemn to death, to be beheaded;* formerly also *in* a fine or forfeiture.
5. To doom to punishment in the world to come, to damn.
6. *fig.* To doom or devote to some (unkind) fate or condition; in *pass.* to be doomed by fate *to* some condition or *to do* something.
7. To adjudge or pronounce forfeited, as a prize of war, smuggled goods, etc.
9. To pronounce incurable, to give up.
10. Of a door or window: To close or block up. (Cf. Fr. *condemner une porte, une fenêtre.*)

Doom, punishment, penalty, forfeiture, fate, blockage. A prize of war, an incurable: something given up. One's life radically not one's own. To be condemned is to be made a thing of. A thing whose shame is publicly perceived, whose punishment is seen as being somehow for the public good. Condemnation: a sign of the range of possibilities implied in loss of freedom.

To be free of condemnation, then, is to be extravagantly set free.

From the loudness and heaviness and banishment of accusation, the threat of stones, physical harm, of violent death. Set free and shown the possibility of the lightness of forgiveness. A freedom born of a refusal of mastery, a refusal to invoke the privilege of law. "Neither will I . . . I will not."

Jesus' last words to her insist upon her changing her life: "Sin no more." So, then, there is an ethical imperative, but it is large, unspecific, privately understood. There is no mention of what are known as sins of the flesh; what she must move from is a larger and less specific darkness.

The next words in this chapter of John: "I am the light of the world."

10

The Blessed

"Blessed are the poor in spirit, for theirs is the kingdom of heaven.

"Blessed are those who mourn, for they shall be comforted.

"Blessed are the meek, for they will inherit the earth.

*"Blessed are those who hunger and thirst for righteousness,
    for they will be filled.*

"Blessed are the merciful, for they will receive mercy.

"Blessed are the pure in heart, for they will see God.

"Blessed are the peacemakers, for they will be called children of God.

*"Blessed are they who are persecuted for righteousness' sake, for theirs is
    the kingdom of heaven.*

*"Blessed are you when people revile you and persecute you and utter all
    kinds of evil against you falsely on my account. Rejoice and be glad,
    for your reward is great in heaven, for in the same way they persecuted
    the prophets who were before you."* MATTHEW 5:3–10

FOR MANY DAYS, I write and rewrite these words by hand and then I am paralyzed. Struck dumb. Afraid to write. Silenced by the depth of my attachment to them, silenced at the example of sheer moral greatness and the sense that after these words there is, perhaps should be, nothing to say.

What kind of life, what kind of living is suggested by the Beatitudes? Perhaps equally important, what virtues are not mentioned . . . elided, simply left out?

Most striking: the bourgeois virtues. There is nothing about honesty, keeping your word, paying your debts, placing yourself in the right place in relation to authority or hierarchy. Mercy, peacemaking, poverty of spirit, purity of heart (the body is not mentioned here). The sexually well-behaved are not given a place.

A pastel palette, tender shades, quiet tones. A world that is safer and more generous. A world that honors the inner intention more than the outward achievement.

THE TRUMPETS, THE PRIMARY COLORS, enter only with the mention of a hunger and thirst for righteousness, a willingness to suffer persecution for its sake. In some translations, "righteousness" is rendered "justice."

When I complained to a wise friend that it was impossible to live up to all the Beatitudes—how can you be both meek and hungering for justice—she told me no one was meant to live up to all of them, that was the glory of them. There were so many, they allowed for many different types of people to be blessed. A refusal then, of singularity. An insistence on a multiplicity of ways. Ways of living, ways of being blessed.

Some translators substitute "Happy" for "Blessed." This will never do. I do not know how to finish a sentence beginning with "I" and including the word "Jesus." But I know that I want the relationship to have less to do with happiness than the selection, protection, and exaltation the word "blessing" implies.

BLESS-ED.

Blest.

Is it a state like being knighted, in that some honor has been bestowed, or is the emphasis not on the bestowal but on the once and for all sheathing of the nature in a state that cannot be compromised or changed? A kind of genius impervious to loss?

The reception of the gift or the gift itself?

AND TO SUCH GIFT what is the right response? What words does one say after "I"? And how would we begin to know ourselves in relation to the Blessing One? A grace said before meals at a Cambridge college is "May the blessed one bless us." But who is the blessed one? And who are we?

When I try to speak of the Beatitude that is most dear to me, "Blessed are they who mourn, for they will be comforted," I stop in my tracks, because any start I make is, I know, a false one. For one thing, it seems radically unlike the others. The other Beatitudes extol moral qualities, and unlike the rewards attached to the other Beatitudes, which seem otherworldly, this one is very concrete. The reward of mourning is comfort, consolation.

But clearly, mourning is not a moral act. To mourn is to mark. It is, in this, related to the artist's work. A kind of making. A making of

85

something of the nothing caused by loss of the beloved. It is simply an act of deep human connection. A useless act, an act without a product. Perhaps even an obsessional one. And to place it beside the making of peace, the hunger for justice, the habit of mercy, is in some ways disconcerting. It is, once again, a refusal on Jesus' part of the straight and strictly defined in favor of the deep movements of the heart.

But should a person of faith be a person of mourning? Shouldn't we believe that the dead are at the bosom of Abraham, or in the hands of God? Perhaps one reason I treasure these words so is that one of my most important identities is that of a perpetual mourner. Every day of my life, I mourn the loss of my beloved father, who died when I was seven years old. And my pious relatives said that I mustn't be sad because my father was in a better place, it was God's will that he called him to himself. They told me that I was wrong to mourn. But I knew that it was they who were wrong. I knew that their refusal to allow me to acknowledge the terribleness of my loss was a kind of lying. A lying about the enormity of loss, an enormity born of love. And the duty to mark it.

I try to understand the place of these words in my life. I write: "It is because of these words that I . . . " That I what? "That I am drawn to Jesus," "that I am compelled by Jesus." These statements are unsatisfying, insufficient, thin. I am drawn to Proust, to Bach, to Bellini, to Colette and Marlon Brando and Oscar Romero and Nelson Mandela. I am compelled by my love for my children. By an urge to write, by delights of friendship and sexual love. But the thing I am in relation to the speaker of the words "Blessed are they who mourn, for they shall be comforted" is different from those other impulses. I begin to write, "If Jesus had said only these words, I . . . " and then I don't know where to go. The words that should follow the "I," that should explain or amplify the "I," are all wrong. "If Jesus had written only these words I . . . " What? Would love him? No, that's not it, not enough. "Would be a follower of his"? I don't like the military tones, the suggestion of brainwashing.

To BLESS THE ACT, the practice, the vocation of mourning suggests an amplitude of understanding, a richness of humanity, of human imagination, that creates in me the impulse I can only name as worship. To say yes: for this I will try to change my life. And more: without this I would not know who I am.

II

The Problem of Jesus: Reading Through Anger, Confusion, Disappointment, Loss

THERE ARE AT LEAST as many good reasons for being appalled by Jesus as there are for being drawn to him. For calling him a liar or a madman, a malign influence in human history, at whose bloody feet can be laid the blame for the Crusades, the Inquisition, or the Holocaust. Or from an aesthetic perspective, the perspective of a lover of beauty and pleasure, lover of Plato and of Plato's Athens, for accusing Jesus of leaching the world of richness, for invoking Swinburne's words, "Thou hast conquered, O pale Galilean; the world has grown grey from thy breath."

And so, of course, one identifies with and envies the bowdlerizing Jefferson. I like thinking of Jefferson, his bewigged, pigtailed head (or did he take his wig off for what might have been sweaty labor—and do we see, rather, an unkempt redhead?), president of the ridiculously young United States, tall, lanky, fifty-plus years old, in shirtsleeves, intent on the pages he is to ravage, taking a pair of scissors in his hands, the delicious shush shush of the scissors on the heavy rag paper, leaving behind him gaps in the text, letting the Enlightenment through, and the silver air of the newly dawning nineteenth century, the air of postrevolutionary America and France. Looking forward to an age in which there would be no more bloodshed, only rationality and moral behavior. And he will see to it that Jesus, decoupled from magic and mystery, and "leaving out everything relative to his personal history and character, this Jesus, a walking tablet of the law, will be our guide."*

---

* Bruce Braden, ed., "Ye Will Say I Am No Christian": The Thomas Jefferson/John Adams Correspondence on Religion, Morals, and Values (Amherst, N.Y.: Prometheus Books, 2006), pp. 99–100.

But what does he do with the residuum? With the spoiled books, the incarnation of the unacceptable? Does he burn them? Bury them? Hide them away? They were costly and he was a lover of books, the creator of a great private library, which he sold to replace the Library of Congress, whose destruction by the British so enraged him that, according to his biographer, he suggested paying incendiaries in London to set British buildings afire in return.

It is tempting, then, to speculate: did he take pleasure in the blatant destructiveness of such an act, joy in it as a sadistic thrill, a bibliophile's black mass?

The pleasure of this kind of destruction and re-creation is connected to the pain and difficulty of a reading which attempts to be complete. It is this pain, or painfulness, that makes all of us secret sharers of Thomas Jefferson's enterprise. But what is the nature of the pain? Like everything connected with a reading of the Gospels, the category is singular, unlike that which attaches to other kinds of reading.

There is a kind of pain when a beloved author displays attitudes that are heinous: Dostoyevsky's or Eliot's anti-Semitism comes to mind. But my distress at Dostoyevsky's anti-Semitism doesn't suggest that there should be a different way to live my life, or that in loving *The Brothers Karamazov* or the *Four Quartets* I was a fool. The pain comes from the singularity of the figure of Jesus: if, for certain important years, one believed he was God, that his words were the words of salvation, that not believing them could lead to eternal damnation, and that he died for you, that he would have died for you singularly if you had been the only person in the world—how can you experience recoil from his words without fear and shame? For this kind of reader of the Gospels, Jesus becomes both Dostoyevsky and Prince Mishkin, Eliot and Tiresias—and the God who cannot be wrong.

. . .

EVEN IF WE READERS of the twenty-first century would be Jeffersons in our desire for a less painful and less problematic text, many of us lack his confidence, and we have learned the price of his blind spots. To be a postmodern is to be, above all, aware of the partiality and incompleteness of our knowledge, and of the horrors that have come about from what we have not seen, could not see, or failed to see. It may not be an entirely good thing for the world that we do not feel free to begin sentences with "All men," as in "all men are created equal." But we simply can't. For one thing, we understand that the words are a lie: all men didn't even mean all men, it meant only white men, to say nothing of women. But "all men are created equal," is not a statement that can be proved by scientific evidence. It is no less a leap of faith than "He died, was buried, and rose on the third day." Like many people of faith, we say we believe "all men are created equal," but we don't live, we probably don't even want to live, as if it were true.

And which of us would be sure that, in Jefferson's words, we could "pick out the diamonds in the dung heap"? Isn't it one of the limits of Jefferson and his Enlightenment cohorts that they were so insistent on denying the importance of the dung? After all, without dung there would be no nourishment, no life. You can't eat diamonds.

I think one reason I prefer Jesus to Jefferson is that he understands there's no point in the separation. With Jesus, the mixed lot of humanness, the paradox of our nature, is, rather than being lamented, insisted upon, named and renamed.

So how do we as readers reject the Jeffersonian temptation? How do we read without a pair of scissors or a shovel or a match? How can we read the words that are there, all of them, and not even succumb to the temptation of a linguistic fudging or contortions that reduce the impact of actions prompted by an understanding, or misunderstanding, of these semiotic marks?

And how much learning is enough for what Virginia Woolf would call a common reader? If you are untrained in scholarly or hermeneutic techniques, can you believe you have a right to read critically? What would this kind of critical reading be when we understand that, even more radically than any other kind of reading, it is a reading in which innocence is impossible because the words have been inscribed on the soft wax of our consciousnesses long before we were old enough for the habit of critical reading? And when there remains, more deeply felt than for any other text, a yearning for an uninterpreted, an uninterpretable text? Could there be a reading that includes the understanding that my desired text may not be yours, yet with a determination not to cut out the nasty bits, not to create our own morocco-bound edition of the Gospel according to ourselves?

This may not be possible. But I want to begin at least acknowledging the problem: the problem of a confrontation with a complicated character, to whom I owe at least the quality of reading I would give to Antigone or to King Lear. Because "my" Jesus leaves a lot out. And my Jesus certainly is not Thomas Jefferson's. Some things I treasure are left in the cut-up books he would describe as trash. And some things he included—the anti-Jewish passages, for example—I find horrifying. What I wish to do now is to read, acknowledging my bafflement, enduring, examining, exploring my horror, my outrage, my sense of disappointment and betrayal. My grief.

1

The Problem
of Miracles

That evening they brought to him many who were possessed with demons; and he cast out the spirits with a word, and cured all who were sick. This was to fulfill what had been spoken through the prophet Isaiah, "He took our infirmities and bore our diseases."

MATTHEW 8:16–17

§

As he walked along, he saw a man blind from birth. His disciples asked him, "Rabbi, who sinned, this man or his parents, that he was born blind?" Jesus answered, "Neither this man nor his parents sinned; he was born blind so that God's works might be revealed in him. We must work the works of him who sent me while it is day; night is coming when no one can work. As long as I am in the world, I am the light of the world." When he had said this, he spat on the ground and made mud with the saliva and spread the mud on the man's eyes, saying to him, "Go, wash in the pool of Siloam" (which means Sent). Then he went and washed and came back able to see. The neighbors and those who had seen him before as a beggar began to ask, "Is this not the man who used to sit and beg?" Some were saying, "It is he." Others were saying, "No, but it is someone like him." He kept saying, "I am the man." But they kept asking him, "Then how were your eyes opened?" He answered, "The man called Jesus made mud, spread it on my eyes, and said to me, 'Go to Siloam and wash.' Then I went and washed and received my sight." They said to him, "Where is he?" He said, "I do not know."

They brought to the Pharisees the man who had formerly been blind. Now it was a sabbath day when Jesus made the mud and opened his eyes. Then the Pharisees also began to ask him how he had received his sight. He said to them, "He put mud on my eyes. Then I washed, and now I see." Some of the Pharisees said, "This man is not from God, for he does not observe the sabbath." But others said, "How can a man who is a sinner perform such signs?" And they were divided. So they said again to the blind man, "What do you say about him? It was your eyes he opened." He said, "He is a prophet."

The Jews did not believe that he had been blind and had received his sight until they called the parents of the man who had received his sight and asked them, "Is this your son, who you say was born blind? How now then does he see?" His parents answered, "We know that this is our son, and that he was born blind; but we do not know how it is that he sees, nor do we know who opened his eyes. Ask him; he is of age. He will speak for himself." His parents said this because they were afraid of the Jews; for the Jews had already agreed that anyone who confessed Jesus to be the Messiah would be put out of the synagogue. Therefore his parents said, "He is of age, ask him."

So for the second time they called the man who had been blind, and they said to him, "Give glory to God! We know that this man is a sinner." He answered, "I do not know whether he is a sinner. One thing I do know, that though I was blind, now I see." They said to him, "What did he do to you? How did he open your eyes?" He answered them, "I have told you already, and you would not listen. Why do you want to hear it again? Do you also want to become his disciples?" Then they reviled him, saying, "You are his disciple, but we are disciples of Moses. We know that God has spoken to Moses, but as for this man, we do not know where he comes from." The man answered, "Here is an astonishing thing! You do not know where he comes from, and yet he opened my eyes. We know that God does not listen to sinners, but he does listen to one who worships him and obeys his will. Never since the world began has it been heard that anyone opened the eyes of a person born blind. If this man were not from God, he could do nothing." They answered him, "You were born entirely in sins, and are you trying to teach us?" And they drove him out.

Jesus heard that they had driven him out, and when he found him, he said, "Do you believe in the Son of Man?" He answered, "And who is he, sir? Tell me, so that I may believe in him." Jesus said to him, "You have seen him, and the one speaking with you is he." He said, "Lord, I believe." And he worshipped him. Jesus said, "I came into the world for judgment so that those who do not see may see, and those who do see may become blind." Some of the Pharisees near him heard this and said to him, "Surely we are not blind, are we?" Jesus said to them, "If you were blind, you would not have sin. But now that you say, 'We see,' your sin remains."　　　JOHN 9:1–41

❧

Peter got out of the boat, started walking on the water, and came toward Jesus. But when he noticed the strong wind, he became frightened, and beginning to sink, he cried out, "Lord, save me!" Jesus immediately reached out his hand and caught him, saying to him, "You of little faith, why did you doubt?"

MATTHEW 14:29–31

❧

Some people brought a blind man to him and begged him to touch him. He took the blind man by the hand and led him out of the village; and when he had put saliva on his eyes and laid his hands on him, he asked him, "Can you see anything?" And the man looked up and said, "I can see people, but they look like trees, walking." Then Jesus laid his hands on his eyes again; and he looked intently and his sight was restored, and he saw everything clearly. Then he sent him away to his home, saying, "Do not even go into the village."

MARK 8:22–26

❧

Now in Jerusalem by the Sheep Gate there is a pool, called in Hebrew Bethzatha, which has five porticoes. In these lay many invalids—blind, lame, and paralyzed. One man was there who had been ill for thirty-eight years. When Jesus saw him lying there and knew that he had been there a long time, he said to him, "Do you want to be made well?" The sick man answered him, "Sir, I have no one to put me into the pool when the water is stirred up, and while I am making my way, someone else steps down ahead of me." Jesus said to him, "Stand up, take your mat and walk." At once the man was made well, and he took up his mat and began to walk.   JOHN 5:2–9

❧

Then some people came, bringing to him a paralyzed man, carried by four of them. And when they could not bring him to Jesus because of the crowd, they removed the roof above him; and after having dug through it, they let down the mat on which the paralytic lay.   MARK 2:3–4

❧

Now a certain man was ill, Lazarus of Bethany, the village of Mary and her sister Martha. Mary was the one who anointed the Lord with perfume and wiped his feet with her hair; her brother Lazarus was ill. So the sisters sent a message to Jesus, "Lord, he whom you love is ill." But when Jesus heard it, he said, "This illness does not lead to death; rather it is for God's glory, so that the Son of God may be glorified through it." Accordingly, though Jesus loved Martha and her sister and Lazarus, after having heard that Lazarus was ill, he stayed two days longer in the place where he was.

Then after this he said to the disciples, "Let us go to Judea again. . . . Our friend Lazarus has fallen asleep, but I am going there to awaken him." The disciples said to him, "Lord, if he has fallen asleep, he will be all right." Jesus, however, had been speaking about his death, but they thought that he was referring merely to sleep. Then Jesus told them plainly, "Lazarus is dead. For your sake I am glad I was not there, so that you may believe. But let us go to him." . . .

When Jesus arrived, he found that Lazarus had already been in the tomb four days. Now Bethany was near Jerusalem, some two miles away, and many of the Jews had come to Martha and Mary to console them about their brother. When Martha heard that Jesus was coming, she went and met him, while Mary stayed at home. Martha said to Jesus, "Lord, if you had been here, my brother would not have died. But even now I know that God will give you whatever you ask of him." Jesus said to her, "Your brother will rise again." Martha said to him, "I know that he will rise again in the resurrection on the last day." Jesus said to her, "I am the resurrection and the life. Those who believe in me, even though they die, will live, and everyone who lives and believes in me will never die. Do you believe this?" She said to him, "Yes, Lord, I believe that you are the Messiah, the Son of God, the one coming into the world."

When she had said this, she went back and called her sister Mary, and told her privately, "The Teacher is here and is calling for you." And when she heard it, she got up quickly and went to him. Now Jesus had not yet come to the village, but was still at the place where Martha had met him. The Jews who were with her in the house, consoling her, saw Mary get up quickly and go out. They followed her because they thought that she was going to the tomb to weep there. When Mary came where Jesus was and saw him, she knelt at his feet and said to him, "Lord, if you had been here, my brother would not have died." When Jesus saw her weeping, and the Jews who came with her also weeping, he was greatly disturbed in spirit and deeply moved. He said, "Where have you laid him?" They said to him, "Lord, come and see." Jesus began to weep. So the Jews said, "See how he loved him!" But some of them said, "Could not he who opened the eyes of the blind man have kept this man from dying?"

Then Jesus, again greatly disturbed, came to the tomb. It was a cave, and a stone was lying against it. Jesus said, "Take away the stone." Martha, the sister of the dead man, said to him, "Lord, already there is a stench because he has been dead four days." Jesus said to her, "Did I not tell you that if you believed, you would see the glory of God?" So they took away the stone. And Jesus looked upward and said, "Father, I thank you for having heard me. I knew that you always hear me, but I have said this for the sake of the crowd standing here, so that they may believe that you sent me." When he had said this, he cried with a loud voice, "Lazarus, come out!" The dead man came out, his hands and feet bound with strips of cloth, and his face wrapped in a cloth. Jesus said to them, "Unbind him and let him go."

JOHN 11:1–44

For a post-Enlightenment consciousness, a mind brought up on the centrality of the scientific method, miracles are a problem. One of Jefferson's major excisions is the airbrushing of the miracles. He simply wasn't having it. His Jesus was not a magician or a trickster; he didn't promise pie in the sky. The prospect enraged Jefferson. His Jesus must reject miracle, like Dostoyevsky's Jesus in the parable of the Grand Inquisitor. Only the despotic Inquisitor insists on the importance of miracle, understanding that it is a way to insure the abrogation of intellectual freedom, to bypass the posture of careful thought in favor of the bended knee.

The prospect of miracles introduces the possibility of a God who can be manipulated by the right words, a critical mass of human pressure, a lobbying of the divine. It forces on us the spectacle of supplication, with its potential for the abject, the hysterical. We prefer to imagine the silent stoic, accepting her fate, than the groveling mendicant, hoping to win the lottery or to be given the secret handshake that will allow him membership into the club of the unimpaired.

These potentials are all the more cringe-inducing as they become incorporated into public display, and connect themselves with money. Televangelists in electric blue polyester suits curing arthritis in the Savior's name, sweating preachers in revival tents, snake handlers, grottoes of hanging crutches, braces, canes: we want to avert our eyes.

Nowhere is this better portrayed than in Fellini's masterpiece, *Nights of Cabiria*. Cabiria, an aging prostitute at the bottom of the Roman food chain, travels with her friends, prostitutes and a pimp, to a pilgrimage site in order that her pimp's uncle, a cripple, and also a pimp and a coke dealer, will be cured. Fellini's camera does not hesitate to linger over toothless crones screaming the name of the Madonna, wild-eyed, beefy macho boys in sunglasses shoving cripples aside in order to be first to kiss the picture of the Virgin. The pimp/coke dealer/crippled uncle asks his pimp nephew if he thinks the Madonna will grace him with a miracle. The nephew says he is sure this will happen if the uncle will put down his crutches. The uncle puts down his crutches and cries out to the Madonna. He falls on his face.

Afterward, during a picnic in which the uncle toothlessly gobbles large hunks of bread and the prostitutes dance to accordion music with newly found johns, Cabiria, having drunk her wine too quickly, shouts in anger at a crowd of pilgrims passing by: "Nothing changed. Nobody changed." And this, to her, is the betrayal. Not that the uncle was unable to walk, but that the hearts of everyone remained untouched.

To believe in miracles is to court a kind of disappointment that very well might name itself as betrayal. It is the betrayal of hope. The betrayal of hope in the invisible. Hope in the overturning of the laws of nature. In the disruption of the straight line of cause.

Thinking of the idea of miracle, I am reminded of Marianne Moore's famous line in relation to poetry, "I too, dislike it." Among the questions I hope never to be asked in a public forum is "Do you believe in miracles?" How would I answer? I would refuse to answer if I were told that I could say only yes or no. I would have to say, it depends on your definition.

The OED defines "miracle" as "an extraordinary and welcome event attributed to divine agency, a remarkable and welcome occurrence, an outstanding example, specimen or achievement." It indicates that the Latin origin is *miraculum*, object of wonder. In the index of Raymond Brown's book *An Introduction to the Gospel of John,* when one looks for the word "miracles," one is directed: "*see* signs." Given these larger definitions and possibilities, what would be implied in saying that we believe? If we say that belief can cover the position "I do not think it is impossible," or "I would like to think it might happen," as opposed to "I know without doubt it is true" . . . then who would not believe in the possibility of miracles? To do so would be a kind of vanity which belies the experience of things occurring inexplicably, beyond our understanding. Also, of things being more wonderful than we would have dreamed. Haven't we all invoked the third of the OED's meanings in the presence of great beauty or mastery: the Piazza Navona, the *Goldberg Variations, King Lear,* a poem by Emily Dickinson, Suzanne Farrell doing a *tour jeté*?

If you confine miracle to an experience synonymous with faith healing, I wouldn't say, "I don't believe." If I were being honest, I would have to say, "I don't like to think about it." For one thing, the whole spectacle is so often embarrassing.

With her uncompromising eye, Flannery O'Connor presents us with a version of this kind of healer in her story "Greenleaf."

> . . . she cut all the morbid stories out of the newspaper. . . . She took these to the woods and dug a hole and buried them and fell on the ground and mumbled and groaned for an hour or so, moving her huge arms back and forth and finally just lying down flat . . . her expression was as composed as a bulldog's. She swayed back and forth on her hands and knees and groaned, "Jesus, Jesus . . . Oh Jesus, stab me in the heart!" . . . and she fell back flat in the dirt, a huge human mound . . .

When the respectable Mrs. May interrupts her, she responds, angrily, "You broken my healing. . . . I can't talk to you until I finish."

Sometimes, it seems, people, even quite unappealing types, do make the blind see and the lame walk. Mr. Greenleaf says proudly of his wife, "She cured a man oncet that half his gut was eat out with worms." And even worse, sometimes those who heal do it for money. The difficult aspect of healing is that it doesn't necessarily have an ethical implication: it's about power, not goodness; the connection between the ability to cure and virtue is, at best, oblique. What is the thread that ties Jesus to con artists curing eczema or epilepsy for the camera or the buck? And how do the nature-defying acts of Jesus connect with the stories of mothers who can pick up cars when their babies are trapped beneath? What is the difference between Jesus and a charlatan, Jesus and someone who can tap into mysterious sources of energy which we all might do if the circumstances were right, or if we found the right New Age practice? Is all physical impairment something that could be undone by the power of positive thinking, by a proficiency in self-hypnosis? I understand why Jefferson would prefer to excise the miracles from the Gospels; it avoids some anguishing questions. It makes the world simpler, less mortifying, more clear.

But why I, unlike Jefferson, would not excise Jesus' miracles from the New Testament is that read not literally but as signs, they are compelling ... narratively, humanly. They witness Jesus' acknowledgment of human affliction, and, unlike the televangelists or the priest in Fellini's mega-pilgrimage, they are intensely personal encounters in which transformation of a profound sort occurs. And if we adopt Raymond Brown's indexing, it is a sign of Jesus' concern and solidarity with suffering humanity. Everyone who approaches Jesus in need is responded to, and cured; no one is turned away. In Jesus' encounters with the afflicted, we are given a model of modest accompaniment, a use of power that does not draw attention to itself, that prefers secrecy to acclaim.

This complex and compelling humanity is particularly evident in the story of the blind man from the ninth chapter of the Gospel of John.

The narrative structure of the episode is quite complex. The story of the actual cure is only part of what is going on: it serves as a pretext for a typical Johannine Pharisee-bashing. After the actual cure, there is a series of delaying tactics. New characters are introduced: the parents, instead of being thrilled that their son is cured, seem to want to disavow him. Their fear of the repercussions of association with Jesus overwhelms their joy in their newly sighted son.

But most important is the introduction of a new and critical ethical point. Jesus is insisting that affliction is not a punishment for sin, either of the afflicted or his parents. His disciples asked him, "Rabbi, who sinned, this man or his parents, that he was born blind?" Jesus answered, "neither this man nor his parents sinned." This is a moment of immense liberation for the suffering; it is an insistence that their suffering not be worsened by assuming that it has a moral component, that it is a punishment. But the next words of Jesus, "he was born blind that God's works might be revealed in him. We must work the works of him who sent me," highlight a problem connected with affliction: the possibility that the afflicted are victimized signifiers, that their suffering is used by God for the edification, the education of the healthy, that God intends for some people to suffer so that others might learn. If God loves all his children equally, how can he allow such an inequality of fate? And in bending the knee to such a God, do we bend the knee to a grotesque injustice that ignores the suffering of some in order to make a larger point? But what point is larger than the suffering of the innocent?

Denise Levertov's poem "St. Thomas Didymus" raises this question. The poem links the apostle Thomas's doubts with the episode of the possessed son of the father who says, "Lord, I believe, help thou my unbelief."

> a man whose entire being
> had knotted itself
> into the one tightdrawn question
> Why,
> why has this child lost his childhood in suffering
> why is this child who will soon be a man
> tormented, torn, twisted?
> Why is he cruelly punished
> who has done nothing except be born . . .
> My question was the same . . .

Levertov resolves the question by invoking a realm which is beyond our understanding.

> My question
> not answered but given
> its part
> in a vast unfolding design lit
> by a rising sun.

This vision of a "vast unfolding design" requires, however, a lighting that blocks the image of the suffering child, a blockage that, for many believers, seems the best, perhaps the only option. And, indeed, at the very beginning of the episode of Jesus' curing the blind man, which occurs soon after that of Jesus and the woman taken in adultery, he speaks one of the central metaphors of his self-identification: "I am the light of the world." Is it a light that blinds as well as illuminates?

Having spoken metaphorically, before he encounters the blind man, Jesus then chooses to heal him in a way that is as physical as it could possibly be: he spits on the ground, makes a paste of the saliva-saturated mud, and applies it to the man's eyes.

But another delay occurs: the blind man is not immediately cured; he must go bathe in the pool, whose name we are given in translation, "Sent" (the translation another delay), and then his sight is restored. A nameless "they" bring the blind man, newly sighted, to the Pharisees, and his cure becomes the pretext for the important discussion, reiterated many times in the Gospel and particularly pointedly in John: Is it possible to violate the Sabbath in order to cure the sick? The Pharisees are bound to look like legalistic villains in any such debate. And what follows is in fact quite a lengthy exchange. Newly sighted, the blind man is perhaps newly voluble. He argues with the Pharisees. And he is driven out.

His business with Jesus is not over. Jesus in fact goes after him, and demands from him an acknowledgment of his belief. "Jesus heard that they had driven him out, and when he found him he said, 'Do you believe in the Son of Man?' He answered, 'And who is he, sir? Tell me, so that I may believe in him.' Jesus said to him, 'You have seen him, and the one speaking with you is he.' He said, 'Lord, I believe.' And he worshipped him." The final words of Jesus are a blatant challenge to the Pharisees, issued in the form of a paradox whose meaning is nevertheless transparent. "If you were blind, you would not have sin. But now that you say, 'We see,' your sin remains."

What is blindness metaphoric for? What is inculpable blindness? What is culpable sight?

A great deal is going on here, and the episode is made up of less than a thousand words. Many literary tasks are accomplished: creation of metaphor, a narrative that involves not only a cure but a window into parent/child relations, ethical revelations. We also experience aggressive challenging, and a final paradoxical coup de grâce. If this is a sign, though, what is it a sign of? It is the complexity of the sign that makes it a different order of experience from what might be called a simple cure: from Fellini's pimp's hope to put down his crutches, the faith healer's success with paralyzed or cancer-ridden patients, the pilgrim to Lourdes leaving her wheelchair at the grotto. The reason for the difference is the inclusion of paradox; the upending of expectations. We don't expect the parents of a newly cured child to be resistant, so fearful of authority that they can't even have a minute of rejoicing. Unlike stories of cures that are meant only to demonstrate themselves, or the power of their practitioners, these stories raise as many questions as they answer. They are unsettling as much as they are vessels of hope.

The Biblical scholar Phyllis Trible told me of her experience in a seminar in Japan in which this miracle was being discussed. Two of the members of the seminar were blind men, both converts to Catholicism. One said he became a Christian because of this miracle, because Jesus took the shame out of blindness, and in a culture in which shame was so important, this seemed like a miracle to him. The other blind man said he hated this miracle, because his sight had not been restored to him by Jesus, and that he became a Christian because of Jesus' words on the Cross, "My God, my God, why hast thou forsaken me?"

IT SEEMS STRANGE TO INCLUDE the words "miracle" and "cliché" in the same sentence, but there is a population whose repeated parading (or, rather, totting up) of miracles, the exaggeration, the focus on the grisly details, have flattened the idea of miracles into the tasteless pancake of cliché. For someone like Fellini, oppressed by the absurdity of the promise of miraculous cures and the distressing but irritating spectacle of credulous petitioners, miracles are also a source of comedy. But as critics from Aristotle on have told us, comedy is about the gap between the ideal and the real, and its territory is the body.

If we look at four accounts—the miracle of Peter walking on water (Matthew 14), the lowering of the cripple through the roof (Mark 2), the blind man who is given faulty vision (Mark 8), and the one who never gets his place at the miraculous pool (John 5)—we see that they all include "whoops" moments. A kind of black comedy about the human lot—the W. C. Fields response to affliction.

The blind man thinks men are like trees walking. Back to the drawing board, says Jesus. Peter tells Jesus to tell him to walk on water: then he realizes he's walking on water and says, "Oh, God, I'm walking on water. People can't walk on water. What the hell was I thinking?" The friends of the cripple can't get past the crowd; they are like a group of New Yorkers at a January sale at Loehmann's pushing their way to the front—in this case taking the roof off. And there's the loser paralytic who keeps trying to get to the miraculous pool—but someone always beats him to it. What do the Evangelists have in mind, in including this sort of low-comedy detail? Certainly, it does not add to the majesty of Jesus, the patina of his followers. What is our experience of reading it? What does it add to, or take away from, our understanding of Jesus and his encounters? How can we incorporate God as straight man into our concept of the divine? It makes Jesus, as a character, more like the fallible Greek gods than like the imperturbable and impermeable Yahweh. It reinforces our discomfort with miracle: our sense of the wrongness of it, our unease at the incursion into the natural order. It insists on the possibility of surprise. And of the great or tragic emotions, surprise is not one. So the genre of the Gospels widens because of the glitch moments involved in these miracles. The possibilities for simplification diminish. We are faced with the limits of our ability to take things in, the problem of who we are, the difficulty of living with what is.

But despite their comic elements, all these encounters have a happy ending . . . and Jesus, who is silent, merely a practitioner in these situations, is not difficult to love. But what about the times when he seems to be withholding his power, or using it to make a point about his mastery? When he is holding back his power like a riverboat gambler hiding cards inside his fancy cuffs?

In the story of the raising of Lazarus, for example, Jesus the miracle worker reveals his dark side.

THERE ARE MANY PUZZLING ASPECTS to this event, and aspects of the telling that cause the reader to be confused about Jesus' identity and his powers. Twice we hear the poignant cry "Lord, if you had been here, my brother would not have died." The repetition of the phrase underscores what seems like a willful laggardliness on Jesus' part, a reluctance that is even attached to a number: he stays in the place where he is two extra days. The suggestion that he's doing it to make a point—that he can raise someone from the dead at any time he wants to—seems callous to the point of brutality.

Such hesitation seems particularly odd when one considers the emotional tone of the language by which the event is described, and the gestures that make up the action, the emphasis on Jesus' personal connection to Mary, Martha, and Lazarus. In a later chapter, John 12, it is Mary the sister of Lazarus, rather than a nameless prostitute, who washes Jesus' feet with perfume and dries them with her hair.

Twice in the first paragraph, Jesus' love for this family is explicitly mentioned. And in contrast to Jesus' reluctant hesitancy, both sisters rise up to meet him before he gets to the house. Weeping is mentioned twice: once because the Jews think Mary is going to her brother's tomb for the express purpose of weeping, and, more astonishingly, because (inaugurating centuries of parodic slang) Jesus also weeps. Interestingly, Martha, famous for being the no-nonsense woman of action versus contemplation, is the only one of the three who does not weep.

But what is Jesus weeping for? And when, exactly, does the weeping happen? It is a temporally odd response; it occurs after Mary's accusation: "Lord, if you had been here, my brother would not have died." He sees her weep, and the sight of her and "the Jews who came with her" also weeping, causes him to be "greatly disturbed in spirit and deeply moved." But he only weeps himself when he has literally seen the place where Lazarus has been interred.

Why does he weep then? Is it possible that he needed this proof that his friend was actually dead? And what could tears mean if he knows Lazarus' death is only temporary, and something that is in his power to undo? Or does he? Does he have a moment of doubt in his own capacity to undo the laws of nature? Does he experience a pang of anxiety—an anxiety that is another form of the anger he experiences when the fig tree will not bear fruit out of season—that the inexorability of the physical is outside his range? Or is he weeping for himself, for the prospect of his own death, which by this time he knows is imminent? Or is he weeping at the prospect of death itself?

Is Jesus allowing his friends to suffer—Lazarus by undergoing a literal death, and the sisters by mourning the loss of their beloved brother—in order to create a spectacle? In order to make a nest for what will be an important metaphor: "I am the resurrection and the life"? In order to make a splash? Raising someone from the dead also raises the ante; this is a level of the miraculous he had not approached before. What are we to make of such showmanship—at the cost of the suffering of people to whom he was close—in order to make a public statement? As he says, "for the sake of the crowd?" This is all the more strange because in most of his other miracles, he insists upon silence.

And what point exactly is he trying to make? That he has a special relationship with God? That God listens to him, and does what he asks? That he himself is divine? If his divinity includes omniscience, as orthodox theology suggests, certainly he knows that Lazarus will be raised and that quite soon he himself will be put to death. So what, exactly, is the point?

It is difficult not to echo the sentiments of the consoling Jews who say, "Could not he who opened the eyes of the blind have kept this man from dying?" The whole question of miracles raises a larger one: if Jesus cures some, why not all? Why not with one stroke erase the whole phenomenon of affliction? Why not ask the Father to mend broken nature so that blindness, lameness, possession, will cease to plague humankind? Or are we meant to believe that suffering has meaning . . . and that some sufferings are more meaningful than others?

It is nearly impossible to look on suffering—uncured, untouched by miracle—and not to raise the fist and ask, "Why not?" Why not my brother, my father, my suffering child? "If he could cure the blind . . . why not?"

Jesus' response is the response of tears. Incomprehensible, paradoxical, perhaps theatrical, perhaps self-serving and manipulative tears.

The story of Lazarus has a power that is not that of realistic fiction and is not that of metaphor. Nor is it the power of myth or tale: we are expected to believe that it happened in real time in a real place. It is the power of a story that unfolds before us and in its unfolding must leave the reader troubled.

. . .

ON THE QUESTION OF MIRACLES, I am, I think, more like the apocryphal Neapolitan cabdriver who explains his failure to stop at red lights by the phrase *"solo un consiglio"*—it's only a suggestion. But a suggestion of what?

A suggestion, perhaps, of transformation. Because miracles are nothing if not a sign of transformation. But we never see the cured ones after the moment of their cure. In Levertov's poem, the speaker, Thomas, makes this point: "no one / dwells on the gratitude, the astonished joy / the swift / acceptance and forgetting. / I did not follow / to see their changed lives."

WHAT WOULD WE HAVE if we had a Gospel without miracles? It would be narrative inevitably tied to nature. Stripped of the inexplicable. With such a Gospel, we are preserved from disappointment. From the shame of credulity. From the pain of our inability to answer the question: What kind of love is this, that does not intervene in suffering that seems endless, random, and unearned? The inexplicable reality that Jesus healed some afflicted people whom he met, but his appearance on the earth would seem to have changed nothing in the economy of human suffering. A central belief in Christianity is that, in sharing human suffering, Jesus gave it meaning. His suffering, however, was chosen by him—he acceded to it in the dark garden—whereas human affliction, unbidden, often degrades the sufferer past the point of her ability to make meaning. The parade of human misery in its endlessly various forms has not been slowed or stopped or thinned or, it would seem, even diverted by the historical fact of Jesus walking on the earth.

Cabiria's cry echoes in our ears. "Nothing changed."

2

The Problem of
Asceticism:
Do We Want to
Live Like This?

"Do not worry about your life, what you will eat, or about your body, what you will wear. For life is more than food, and the body more than clothing. Consider the ravens: they neither sow nor reap, they have neither storehouse nor barn, and yet God feeds them. Of how much more value are you than the birds! And can any of you by worrying add a single hour to your span of life? If then you are not able to do so small a thing as that, why do you worry about the rest? Consider the lilies, how they grow: they neither toil nor spin; yet I tell you, even Solomon in all his glory was not clothed like one of these." LUKE 12:22–27

❧

You received without payment; give without payment. Take no gold, or silver, or copper in your belts, no bag for your journey, or two tunics, or sandals, or a staff; for laborers deserve their food.

MATTHEW 10:8–10

❧

*But truly I tell you that unless a grain of wheat falls into the earth
and dies, it remains a single grain. But if it dies it bears much
fruit.* JOHN 12:24

❧

*Those who want to save their life will lose it, and those who lose
their life for my sake will save it. What does it profit them if they
gain the whole world, but lose or forfeit themselves?*

LUKE 9:24–25

❧

*While he was still speaking to the crowds, his mother and his
brothers were standing outside, wanting to speak to him. Someone
told him, "Look, your mother and your brothers are standing
outside, wanting to speak to you." But to the one who had told him
this, Jesus replied, "Who is my mother, and who are my brothers?"
And pointing to his disciples, he said, "Here are my mother and
my brothers! For whoever does the will of my Father in heaven is
my brother and sister and mother."* MATTHEW 12:46–50

❧

*"Do you think that I have come to bring peace to the earth? No, I
tell you, but rather division! From now on five in one household
will be divided, three against two and two against three; they will*

be divided: father against son and son against father, mother against daughter and daughter against mother, mother-in-law against her daughter-in-law and daughter-in-law against mother-in-law." LUKE 12:51–53

"Whoever comes to me and does not hate father and mother, wife and children, brothers and sisters, yes, and even life itself, cannot be my disciple." LUKE 14:26

To another he said, "Follow me." But he said, "Lord, first let me go and bury my father." But Jesus said to him, "Let the dead bury their own dead; but as for you, go and proclaim the kingdom of God." LUKE 9:59–60

THE PROBLEM OF ASCETICISM is a different order from the problem of miracles. What is one to make of assertions that seem life-hating, dualistic in a way that names the body as a problem to be overcome, a curse, a stumbling block placed in our road by a God who demands only that we get over the natures we have been given?

Life. Liberty. The pursuit of happiness.

Where does Jesus fit in this triangle, or troika? Of the three, life would seem to be the easiest to attach to him. Jesus tells us he has come that we may have life and life more abundantly. Liberty: a public category, a category of state—Jesus has said that the truth will set us free, not give us liberty: a freedom that is personal, not an affair of the polis. Nevertheless, it is possible to find justification in the Gospels for the pursuit of liberty, or liberation. But happiness? Not a word about it can be found in the New Testament—and as I have noted when speaking of the Beatitudes, the translations that substitute "Happy are the . . . " for "Blessed are the . . . " fall dead on the page, the ear.

Jesus does not seem to be about happiness. And certainly not about pleasure. Except for the moment when he luxuriates in having his feet bathed, he presents an ideal of conduct that can only be thought of as ascetic.

There is a kind of asceticism that Jesus advocates that seems, if difficult, then entirely desirable: a program for simplifying life, for cutting out excess and glut. This is expressed most famously in the lilies of the field passage from Luke in which Jesus urges against material anxiety. He consistently exhorts his followers not to concern themselves with wealth . . . the famous rich man and the eye of the needle trope comes immediately to mind. I have always been puzzled by the Gospel of Prosperity folks . . . it seems to me they were reading a different book from me. The Jesus I encounter in the pages of the Gospel is clear that prosperity is not the Way, the Truth, and the Life.

And his advice to his disciples about how they are to receive food, clothing, shelter, and payment, would seem to be a safeguard against corruption and the oppression of the faithful by those who are meant to serve them.

These prospects offer a possibility of refreshment, as one is pleased and refreshed by Japanese interior décor, a desert landscape, the Antarctic, a drink of water and lemon. They are a salutary corrective at a time in which, not so long ago, the leader of the free world felt it right to suggest that the best response to tragedy is shopping. And certainly, the renunciation of what is harmful, distracting, even unessential is a component of every spiritual tradition, a part of not only spiritual but psychological maturity.

Nineteen hundred years after the writers of the Gospels, Emily Dickinson created haunting images of the visionary powers of renunciation: rejection of the inferior sight for the ultimately valuable one.

Renunciation—is a piercing Virtue—
The letting go
A Presence—for an Expectation—
Not now—
The putting out of Eyes—
Just Sunrise—
Lest Day—
Day's Great Progenitor—
Outvie—

Renunciation—is the Choosing
Against itself—
Itself to justify
Unto itself—
When larger function—
Make that appear—
Smaller—that Covered Vision—Here—

"Piercing," "putting out of Eyes." These images clearly recall the words of Zechariah quoted by John in relation to Jesus: "They will look upon him whom they have pierced" and Jesus' own words. "If your eye offends you, pluck it out." But in choosing these images, Dickinson exposes the inevitable aggression that is part and parcel of the ascetic impulse—an aggression none the less real for being directed against oneself, "the Choosing / Against itself," or played out in the conflict between nature and the invisible transcendent, "Lest Day—/ Day's Great Progenitor—/ Outvie," a particularly anguishing conflict for one who loved nature as passionately as Dickinson. And she touches on the possibilities of solipsism involved in the prospect of renunciation, "the Choosing / Against itself—/ Itself to justify / Unto itself." But who would not endure these minor discomforts to win the ultimate prize of true vision?

In the same way that one can view renunciation as a positive activity, it is similarly possible to value the perception that death is not only inevitable, but sometimes a desirable choice.

ISN'T IT A QUESTION that needs to be considered: What is lost in life if life itself is considered the highest good? Isn't it possible that meaningfulness is inexorably connected to the possibility of self-sacrifice? Unless one can imagine giving up one's life for something or someone else, then nothing is more important than survival. We live to live. We are no better than animals, who, in seeking only their own survival, do not seek meaning. If we live for survival, what, really, are we living for? The words of Jesus that touch on these ideas, then, are challenging, but we can at least imagine them as having a possible beneficent component.

The problem occurs when Jesus appears to see death as preferable to life. Not because other life is being enabled and its only price is death, but because, as a category, death seems more desirable. This posture seems to me more dangerous than the clearly metaphorical "if your eye offends you, cut it out." It can, of course, be understood as an example of the kind of exaggerated rhetoric typical of the Hebrew prophets. As someone who was brought up hearing threats like "Put that down or I'll break your arm and beat you with the bloody stump," I think I know better than to take some kinds of language literally.

The hyperbole whose root is the Hebrew prophets seems much less dangerous to me than the dualism, which we most often find in passages like the one in the sixth chapter of John, "It is the spirit that gives life; the flesh is useless." Of all the Evangelists, John is most formed by the Hellenic tradition, which, unlike the Hebrew tradition, links the body with death, the spirit with life. It is a quick trip from this life-denial to the darkness of Counter-Reformation morbidity, which brought with it a tonality that shifted quickly from solemnity to sadomasochism.

DOES RENUNCIATION OF AN EXCESSIVE attachment to the flesh necessarily require hatred of it? "What is prized by human beings is an abomination in the sight of God," Jesus says in the sixteenth chapter of Luke.

Does that mean everything, one wants to ask in exasperation? Everything prized by human beings? Does that include Bernini and Bach? Chartres? Penicillin? Would the world really be better without these things? Surely sometimes some people in the world have prized the right things for the right reasons ... Or have we all been all wrong all the time? One reads Luke's version of the Beatitudes with a thudding of the spirit. "Woe to you who are laughing now, for you will mourn and weep." One longs for Matthew's more generous version. When I read his words, I can't help but remember the holiday gatherings of my large extended family. Whenever my cousin and I seemed to be having a good time, seemed to be "laughing too much," we were separated with the warning "This laughing will end in tears." Years later, my cousin told me it was his first indication that maybe grown-ups weren't always right, because, as he said, sometimes laughing just ended up in more laughing.

And do we have to believe that happiness is always bad for the character? Were the Puritans the beau ideal of human conduct? Aren't the Salem witch trials a predictable outcome of such deprivation? "I live in a constant endeavor to fence against the infirmities of ill health, and other evils of life, by mirth; being firmly persuaded that every time a man smiles—but much more so when he laughs, that it adds something to this fragment of life." These words were written by Laurence Sterne, a clergyman of the Church of England, a devout and famously charitable Christian who also happened to write one of the funniest books in the world; those words were found in the introduction to the first volume of *Tristram Shandy*. At another time, he also said, "I am always more generous when I am in love." Do we have to believe that Cotton Mather and John Calvin were more right about the human condition than Laurence Sterne? What is the good of hatred of the world? In what context is hatred of life itself desirable?

And if this radical detachment from the things of this world seems a case of fanatical and destructive overstatement, what are we to make of Jesus' insistence that personal relations are not important? We can imagine a cutting off from pleasure as possibly leading to moral growth or a detachment that makes imaginative acts more possible—but can we imagine a good world in which connection to other humans is considered not only beside the point but in the way?

The saccharine and claustrophobic invocation of "family values" by the religious right makes Jesus' continuous cold-shouldering of his kin seem downright appealing. It is certainly an antidote to provincialism, to a fear of the outside world. And indeed, it has been very important for many people whose lives have been distorted by family relations—particularly, for example, victims of abuse—to remove "the family" from its unassailable, privileged position in the pantheon of the good. But Jesus sounds like a teenage brat when people try to tell him to acknowledge those he was born of. The incident is repeated by Matthew, Mark, and Luke; it must have seemed to them central to Jesus' teachings.

Jesus not only advocates detachment from familial ties, he insists that one of his goals is to destroy them, to break apart family connections. These assertions go far beyond a healthy independence; the tone is violently aggressive. What happened to the fellow with the little kiddies on his lap? Was that only for losers, for people not really taking their primary place in the kingdom? What would this harshness enable that would lead to the purification, the perfection, the salvation of humankind?

The most disturbing instance of this harshness, for me, occurs in Matthew, and is repeated in Luke, when the disciple asks if he can wait to follow Jesus until he buries his father.

"Let me go and bury my father." . . . "Let the dead bury their own dead."

The syntactic parallelism makes the response even more shocking. "Let me" . . . "Let the." Let the dead bury the dead? What can that possibly mean? Can the senior dead prevent the eyes of their juniors from being plucked out by carrion crows? Certainly the task of burying the corruptible and rotting body would seem to be time-sensitive, whereas Jesus will be around for a while. Certainly the grieving son would be able to catch up to him in the next town. And is the mourning son not one of the blessed mourners invoked in Matthew's Beatitudes?

The burial of the dead was a sacred responsibility in the ancient world. Consider Antigone. Can it be that Jesus is taking on the role of Creon the tyrant? Obey my impossible command . . . forget your ties to the beloved dead. "Rebellion against tyrants is obedience to God," said Benjamin Franklin, one of Jefferson's Enlightenment cohort.

To bury the dead might be the most pure of all ethical acts because no reciprocity is possible.

I would have buried my father. I would not have followed Jesus. I would have known that I was right.

3

The Problem of Perfection: Could We Live the Way He Says Even If We Wanted To?

"You have heard that it was said to those of ancient times, 'You shall not murder'; and 'whoever murders shall be liable to judgment.' But I say to you that if you are angry with a brother or sister, you will be liable to judgment; and if you insult a brother or sister, you will be liable to the council, and if you say, 'You fool,' you will be liable to the hell of fire. So when you are offering your gift at the altar, if you remember that your brother or sister has something against you, leave your gift there before the altar and go; first be reconciled to your brother or sister, and then come and offer your gift. Come to terms with your accuser. . . . You have heard that it was said, 'You shalt not commit adultery.' But I say to you that everyone who looks at a woman with lust has already committed adultery with her in his heart. . . . It was also said, 'Whoever divorces his wife, let him give her a certificate of divorce.' But I say to you that anyone who divorces his wife, except on the ground of unchastity, causes her to commit adul-

*tery; and whoever marries a divorced woman commits adul-
tery. . . . . You have heard that it was said, 'An eye for an eye and
a tooth for a tooth.' But I say to you, Do not resist an evildoer.
But if anyone strikes you on the right cheek, turn the other also;
and if anyone wants to sue you and take your coat, give your
cloak as well; and if anyone forces you to go one mile, go also the
second mile. Give to everyone who begs from you, and do not
refuse anyone who wants to borrow from you. You have heard
that it was said, 'You shall love your neighbor and hate your
enemy.' But I say to you, Love your enemies and pray for those
who persecute you, so that you may be children of your Father in
heaven; for he makes his sun rise on the evil and on the good, and
sends rain on the righteous and the unrighteous. For if you love
those who love you, what reward do you have? Do not even the
tax collectors do the same? And if you greet only your brothers
and sisters, what more are you doing than others? Do not even the
Gentiles do the same? Be perfect, therefore, as your heavenly
Father is perfect."* MATTHEW 5:21–48

*"Love your enemies, do good to those who hate you, bless those
who curse you, pray for those who abuse you. If anyone strikes
you on the cheek, offer the other also; and from anyone who takes
away your coat, do not withhold even your shirt. Give to everyone
who begs from you; and if anyone takes away your goods, do not
ask for them again. Do to others as you would have them do to
you. If you love those who love you, what credit is that to you? For
even sinners love those who love them. If you do good to those who*

do good to you, what credit is that to you? . . . Even sinners lend to sinners, to receive as much again. But love your enemies, do good, and lend, expecting nothing in return. Your reward will be great; and you will be children of the most high; for He is kind to the ungrateful and the wicked." LUKE 6:27–35

ONE NIGHT AT DINNER my son, then eighteen, said to me, "I don't want to be a Christian because Jesus says you have to be perfect. I have no interest in perfection; I think it's a bad thing to try to get."

I have a dream about me and Flannery O'Connor. We are on a panel together. Her hair is immaculate, she is wearing a dress with a starched white Peter Pan collar; her notes are on index cards, held together with a single rubber band. My hair is filthy, my stockings are full of runs, my shoes are filthy, my notes are in disarray. She says to me, "The problem with you is you don't believe in perfection." I answer her, "I do believe in perfection, but you think perfection is flawlessness, and I think it's completeness."

A friend's mother says to her, "Perfect is dead."

My friend's mother, Phyllis Katz, was on the same wavelength as the nineteenth-century poet Gerard Manley Hopkins. His poem "The Habit of Perfection" consistently invokes images of death, or deadness.

Elected Silence, sing to me
And beat upon my whorlèd ear,
Pipe me to pastures still and be
The music that I care to hear.

Shape nothing, lips; be lovely-dumb:
It is the shut, the curfew sent
From there where all surrenders come
Which only makes you eloquent.

Be shellèd, eyes, with double dark
And find the uncreated light:

This ruck and reel which you remark
Coils, keeps, and teases simple sight. . . .

Nostrils, your careless breath that spend
Upon the stir and keep of pride,
What relish shall the censers send
Along the sanctuary side!

Sightless, soundless, scentless—this for Hopkins is Perfection, habitation of the land of death. But what is the relationship between perfection and life?

"Be perfect, therefore, as your heavenly Father is perfect." Jesus says this during the Sermon on the Mount, the same event that produced the Beatitudes. What can he possibly mean by that? Doesn't it seem to be encouraging a kind of self-idolatry? We are not God. Why should we try to model ourselves after a Being to whom we are infinitely inferior?

Nothing in Jesus' diction could be paraphrased by the words "it would be best if" . . . or even "it would be good if." The tone is absolute, and the consequences are as well. His prescriptions are detailed, specific, and unequivocal. They range from the practical to the abstract; sometimes he seems to be advising what could be called prudent behavior, and other times demanding an otherworldly selflessness.

In this passage, we experience an admixture of the impossible but beautiful ideal, some trimming, and some assertions that seem just plain wrong. A human organization not based on power and hierarchy would seem to avoid many of the corruptions and evils of social organization—even if those of us who lived through the sixties came to see that it probably wouldn't work. The ideal of "resisting not evil" has been debated for centuries; it is possible to believe that failing to resist evil results in its triumph—always the figure of Hitler is invoked—but certainly all people of goodwill would prefer nonviolent resistance if we believed that it worked. The choice of violence over nonviolence if both were equally efficacious would be an indication of moral callousness, if not moral heinousness. If we could give without asking to be given equally in return, love from the sheer impulse of loving without asking to be loved back or calculating who loved more and how much and who first . . . how much heartbreak and recrimination would be saved? Isn't it a difficult but desirable goal: to renounce the voluptuous pleasures of anger and grudge-bearing? And how wonderful if we could give up the law of retribution—an eye for an eye, a tooth for a tooth: certainly we have seen the horrid and endlessly vortical effects of this. Do we not inhabit a world where eyes and teeth litter the wayside of history? Are we not eyeless and toothless, or partially sighted gummers at the best? The image of love beyond the judgment of worthiness to love is moving, and Hamlet's "use every man after his desert, and who should 'scape whipping?" is an echo of Jesus' words. Any of us who has ever transgressed—and I am assuming that this includes the whole species—would have to be comforted by the possibility of unearned love. Because how much goodness is enough to earn love? And how much love?

This plane of moral grandeur does not support Jesus during the whole of this passage. His advice on avoiding litigation seems much more pragmatic than idealistic: "Come to terms quickly with your accuser while you are on the way to court with him, or your accuser may hand you over to the judge, and the judge to the guard, and you will be thrown into prison. Truly I tell you, you will never get out until you have paid the last penny." And his high terms about divorce seem irrelevant if the wife is a fornicator, or fornicatress. "It was also said, 'Whoever divorces his wife, let him give her a certificate of divorce.' But I say to you that anyone who divorces his wife, except on the ground of unchastity, causes her to commit adultery; and whoever marries a divorced woman commits adultery." "Except on the ground of unchastity." How to square this with "what God has joined together let no man put asunder?" Or does it mean that the very act of fornication on the part of a woman is a sign that God never put them together? This opens the way for the kind of ethical waffling that the Catholic Church has adopted because it chooses the moral tortuousness of annulment rather than the clarity of divorce. The very tone of the term "what God has joined" would seem to be of a different order of language from "except in the case of." And what about fornicators of the male gender? No provision is made for wives who might want to be divorced from them.

Jesus' insistence that the will and the deed, or even the imagination of the will and the deed, are identical seems cruel to the point of lunacy. Jimmy Carter was ridiculed by everyone who could hold a pen when he confessed to "lusting in his heart." Once again, this is a brutal strike against those who have had temptations against which they have struggled successfully. Certainly the human task of resisting a powerful impulse should be understood as an important part of moral life. I remember a friend of mine, a Christian, telling me a story about discussing a potential adultery with her potential partner, a Jew. In the middle of the discussion she said, "Should we be feeling guilty about this?" He said, "For what? We haven't done anything." She invoked Matthew 5. He told her she was crazy.

Is there really no difference between imagination and action? Suppose we interpolate the story of David and Bathsheba and examine it in the light of Jesus' prescriptions. David sees Bathsheba bathing; he desires her. What would have happened if, desiring her, he prayed, even if unsuccessfully, to banish the image of the beautiful woman from his mind? What if, even praying unsuccessfully, even if the image refused to dislodge itself, he had prayed to God that he not act on his temptation? What if, sweating on his tormented bed, he had overcome his impulse, stayed away from Bathsheba, and not sent Uriah the Hittite off to battle in order to be slain? Wouldn't we consider him morally heroic, and be grateful that life was spared? Would we vilify him for his initial impulse? Or would we praise him for his restraint? (On the other hand, without David's having given in to his impulse, there would have been no Solomon.) The issue of the sinful congress, achieved before marriage, results in a child who dies. But eventually, neither David nor the Jewish people are punished for his transgression: the end result is Solomon in all his glory. If David had plucked his eye out, there would have been no temple. What was required was David's repentance. But Jesus isn't talking about repentance. He is talking about tendencies that attach to humans because of something out of their control. It could be said that these words are just a more extreme version of "Let him who is without sin cast the first stone." Jesus is always hardest on hypocrites. Yet in this harsh statement, no provision is made for the soul in struggle, and the benefits that might accrue from temptation overcome. Jesus seems to be equating sin and temptation. This seems, to say the least, quite strange.

Strange, too, is the lack of moral relativism: Is calling someone a fool really the equivalent of murder? Is insult really homicide? "You have heard that it was said to those of ancient times, 'You shall not murder,' and 'whoever murders shall be liable to judgment.' But I say to you that if you are angry with a brother or sister, you will be liable to judgment; and if you insult a brother or sister, you will be liable to the council; and if you say, 'You fool,' you will be liable to the hell of fire." Those of us who have spared fools the execution we might wish for them, but nevertheless called them fools—is there no difference between us and those who have taken someone's life, once and for all? What can it mean that the same punishment is meted out to a murderer and someone with a quick temper and a sharp tongue?

And what would be the perceived good of creating a set of principles that humans are unable to live up to? I remember a conversation with a German nun I know, whose life is lived as much as any I've observed according to the principles of Gospel service to the poor. We were discussing my discomfort with some of the more violent wishes in the psalms; I said I couldn't go along with expressing the desire that your enemies' children's faces be crushed. She said she was much more comfortable with that sort of thing, which at least was realistic about human darkness, than with the prohibitions of Jesus, which she felt were too far removed from how human beings really are.

Rabbi Abraham Joshua Heschel underscores this difference between Christian and Jewish ethical epistemology. In an essay urging Jews to engage in the public fight for justice, particularly the civil-rights and antiwar movements, he implicitly criticizes the perfectionism of Christian moral thought:

> The Torah has not imposed upon Israel a tyranny of the spirit. On the contrary, the road to the sacred leads through the secular. The spiritual rests upon the carnal. Like "the Spirit that hovers over the face of the water." Jewish living means living according to a system of checks and balances. We are not asked anything that cannot be responded to. We are not told: "Love thy enemy," but "Do not hate him," and positively: "If thou

meet thy enemy's ox or his ass going astray, thou shalt surely bring it back to him again" (Exodus 23:4).

Although there is no celebration of our animal nature, recognition of its right and role is never missing. Judaism does not despise the carnal teaching, on the contrary. "Hide not yourself from your own flesh."*

Is it possible that "perfection" is a mistranslation, or an archaism? If so, it has had a long and effective shelf life. And, once again, even if it can be argued that the words must be contextualized, the text has been long canonized, and most people come to it without commentary. And even if we accept the New English Bible's translation of "Be ye perfect as your heavenly Father is perfect" as "There must be no limit to your goodness, as your heavenly Father's goodness knows no bounds," the standard set is the standard of God.

Even that can lead to moral despair. Sanity involves the creation of boundaries.

The injunction to be perfect is entirely omitted from Jefferson's text.

But there is a certain thrill to the impossible prescription. And isn't it possible that only the vision of the impossible makes the great a possibility? Without the challenge of the impossible, would we be doomed to the mediocre? I force myself to understand that there is a kind of person who does not prefer the injunction "Love your enemies, do good to those who hate you . . . turn the other cheek . . . resist not evil" to what seem to me the comparatively empty calories of

* Abraham Joshua Heschel, "No Time for Neutrality," in *Moral Grandeur and Spiritual Audacity,* edited by Susannah Heschel (New York: Farrar, Straus and Giroux, 1996), p. 19.

"Try to be more kind. Think of those who have less than you." I even have to acknowledge that such people may be devoted to Beethoven and Wallace Stevens. Some of them are my friends. But they are friends from a different tribe. The tribe that has not inscribed over its tents "Be ye perfect."

WOULD I BE HAPPIER without the words "Be ye perfect"?

Would I prefer "Let your love be endless"?

I would prefer either to "Do your best. We're all human." Human, in this definition, means doing a great deal less than what the great among us have done.

The habit of perfection. For Hopkins, it is with an end in sight, either the poet's reward of eloquence, or the faithful servant's reward of a paradisal realm: sweet wind, fresh crust, relish of censers, golden streets, lily-colored clothes. Jesus offers no such enticements. The stakes are this: perfection, or eternal punishment.

But what would such a perfect world be like?

The land of the unliving.

The undead.

4

The Problem of
Apocalypticism

*"So when you see 'the abomination of desolation,' of which the
prophet Daniel spoke, standing in the holy place (let the reader
understand), then those who are in Judea must take to the hills. If
a man is on the roof, he must not come down to fetch his goods
from the house; if in the field, he must not turn back for his coat.
Alas for women with child in those days, and for those who have
children at the breast! Pray that it may not be winter when you
have to make your escape, or Sabbath. It will be a time of great
distress; there has never been such a time from the beginning of
the world until now, and will never be again. If that time of
troubles were not cut short, no living thing could survive; but for
the sake of God's chosen it will be cut short.*

*"Then, if anyone says to you, 'Look, here is the Messiah,' or,
'There he is,' do not believe it. Imposters will come claiming to be
messiahs or prophets, and they will produce great signs and won-
ders to mislead even God's chosen, if such a thing were possible.
See, I have forewarned you. If they tell you, 'He is there in the
wilderness,' do not go out; or if they say, 'He is there in the inner
room,' do not believe it. Like lightning from the east, flashing as
far as the west, will be the coming of the Son of Man.*

"Wherever the corpse is, there the vultures will gather. . . .

"As things were in Noah's days, so will they be when the Son of Man comes. In the days before the flood they ate and drank and married, until the day that Noah went into the ark, and they knew nothing until the flood came and swept them all away. That is how it will be when the Son of Man comes. Then there will be two men in the field; one will be taken, the other left; two women grinding at the mill; one will be taken, the other left.

"Keep awake, then; for you do not know on what day the Lord is to come."   MATTHEW 24:15–42

"Truly I tell you, there are some standing here who will not taste death before they see the Son of Man coming into his kingdom."
          MATTHEW 16:28

"There will be signs in the sun, the moon, and the stars, and on the earth distress among nations confused by the roaring of the sea and the waves. People will faint from fear and foreboding of what is coming upon the world, for the powers of the heavens will be shaken. Then they will see 'the Son of Man coming in a cloud' with power and great glory. Now when these things begin to take place, stand up and raise your heads, because your redemption is drawing near."   LUKE 21:25–28

"But in those days, after that suffering, the sun will be darkened, and the moon will not give its light, and the stars will be falling from heaven, and the powers in the earth will be shaken. Then they will see 'the Son of Man coming in clouds' with great power and glory. Then he will send out the angels, and gather his elect from the four winds, from the ends of the earth to the ends of heaven. . . . Truly I tell you, this generation will not pass away until all these things have taken place." MARK 13:24–30

OCTOBER 14, 1962. The Cuban missile crisis. I am in eighth grade, about to turn thirteen. Kennedy challenges Castro; Castro won't budge. Kennedy delivers an ultimatum. Castro and Khrushchev deliver one of their own: they will blow us up. The entire school, eight hundred children between the ages of six and thirteen, is marched across the street to the church, where we sit and pray all day instead of having ordinary classes. We believe it is the end of the world.

The larger world, the world of newspapers and television and political commentators, reinforced our belief that we were in mortal danger. But the words of the Gospel that we heard every year at the end of November, the beginning of Advent, the dark words echoing the approaching darkness of the year, the dread of the sun's gradual withdrawal, had made the ground fertile for this kind of imagining.

Sitting in our winter coats, too warm perhaps for the first days of fall, or just warm enough if the new cold were seeping up through the stones, we heard the description of the last days from the Gospel of Matthew.

They were thrilling and terrifying, those words, those visions; we were inhabiting darkness and fear: nothing could surprise us, we knew what the signs could be. We would know when the end was approaching but not quite. And we could be wrong. Because one of the terrors of the end time is the terror of confusion: people claiming to be Jesus but who are not. How easy to imagine oneself running from the wilderness to the inner chamber, only to be deceived, again and again, never to find Jesus. The nightmare scene of frantic uncertainty, desperate unknowing. Suppose one was one of the deceived, or worse, one who did not endure? It was very easy to interpolate the prophecy of the deceivers, the confusers, into what we had been told about the tactics of the Communists. We ate up stories of persecuted Eastern European Christians, priests tortured by the Chinese, bamboo under their fingernails. We knew that the Russians were famous for turning families against one another; in our safe beds we practiced ignoring the blandishments of our parents, aunts, and uncles if they seemed to be speaking in the devil's name.

"The abomination of desolation"—I had no idea what it meant but my spine thrummed at the words. Abomination . . . desolation . . . how odd that the two words should be linked: the first a public uncleanness almost beyond language, rendering the object unworthy of love, even of inclusion in the human community. A hot word, a loud word: flame and drum and sword surround it. But desolation: the ultimate solitariness, the coldness of a banishment inflicted by the community, self-inflicted, whose most important characteristic is that it cannot be shared. Sent out into the desert, into an endless night without even the accompaniment of moon and stars.

Abomination . . . desolation . . . it was easy for me to have access to both these things, and although I didn't analyze them intellectually or even consciously, or explore what their proximity might mean, both had a deep resonance in the place of the darkest fears: the fear of what it might really mean to be human, what was in store that we were only keeping, or that was being kept, temporarily at arm's length. Did it suggest that loneliness in itself was hateful? That not to be surrounded by one's kind was a kind of justice: one was alone because one was loathsome? Abominable. Desolate.

My sensual imagination, the part of my mind whose work was the making of images, was made ardent by the dramatic details of the last days. The words were distant, but electrifying, like the stories of the Crusades or the armies of Alexander the Great. They had the appeal of brushing away the everyday and all its problems as paltry and irrelevant.

But Jesus domesticates and personalizes the tone; the last days are both dreadful and familiar; the combination makes us even more afraid. "The one on the housetop must not go down to take what is in the house; the one in the field must not turn back to get a coat." "And woe to those who are with child . . . " I was always worried that I would be pregnant at the end of the world, this was what I fixed on, as I fixed on the fear of not being able to find my mother when the atom bomb struck New York.

For the first time now, quite near the age of sixty, I read the different versions of the Apocalypse of Jesus: read them comparatively rather than hearing them in a church redolent of the approach of winter darkness. Looking closely at Matthew's account, we can see all the elements that make apocalyptic pronouncements so compelling—and so dangerous. The keys to the danger are the words "elect" and "chosen" (Matthew's use of which is later repeated by Mark): "And if those days had not been cut short, no one would be saved; but for the sake of the elect those days will be cut short. . . . And he will send out his angels with a loud trumpet call, and they will gather the elect from the four winds, from one end of heaven to the other."

THE IDEA OF THE ELECT IS, it seems to me, an important element in the popularity of apocalyptic retellings like the Rapture books. The most likely explanation is that we all understand that time is, by its very nature, something that has an end . . . and therefore that there will be an end time, an end of the world. If the world must end, or, put another way, if we must give it up, isn't it easier to contemplate such an eventuality if what is being given over is chaotic, frightening, out of control, if the ending will be colorful and glorious and swift? Such an outcome provides a structure that is necessarily dramatic, a language that is necessarily violent and stark. But it appeals to another and darker part of the human imagination—the desire to be among the saved remnant, to watch from a comfortable perch while others are hurtled to their doom. Because the idea of punishment is inextricably linked with the apocalyptic vision. The twenty-fifth chapter of Matthew, which takes up the apocalyptic narrative after the insertion of the parable of the wise and foolish virgins, and the story of the servants and the talents, situates the punishment that happens at the end time firmly in an ethical context. It is difficult not to say "hurrah" at the prospect of greed and indifference to the poor finally getting its just deserts—but most of us tend to number ourselves among the luxuriantly woolly sheep rather than the poor singed and stinking goats.

There is an additional problem that occurs during a close reading of the apocalyptic passages of the Gospels. It is the problem of time. Although sometimes Jesus is vague about when in time the climactic event will occur, sometimes he seems to be saying that the end of the world is imminent: "Truly I tell you, there are some standing here who will not taste death before they see the Son of Man coming in his kingdom" (Matthew 16:28); "Truly I tell you, this generation will not pass away until all these things have taken place" (Mark 13:30).

This sense of the imminence of the end time was a commonplace among Jesus' contemporaries. But, in fact, the end of the world did not imminently occur. So it would seem Jesus is wrong. What then are we to make of a God who errs, a God who opens his worshippers to the anguish of embarrassment? "Embarrassment," "God"—how to combine these two in a meaningful sentence? It seems Jesus is making a huge mistake. Embarrassing like one of those filthy ranters on the street, barefoot, with a long, unkempt beard and a sandwich board crying on Times Square, "The end is near."

This wouldn't be a problem if we had a concept of God like polytheistic religions'—a god, for example, like Krishna, who is from time to time all too human. But in the Christian God, the God who is attached to Yahweh, the Son of God, the Christ who we have been told is omniscient . . . how do we understand him as a Person of mistakes? How do we understand him as capable of error? As someone who causes us embarrassment? Must we then rethink error? Or do these moments force us to rethink our concept of God? A God who is capable of embarrassing us? A God who can be wrong?

Or did Jesus take on divinity only gradually, piecemeal? When did it hit him? When did it take?

Does Jesus become someone like Shakespeare, or like Socrates, capable of occasional wisdom but not someone to be followed step by step?

And what is lost if we take up this line of thought?

Certainty. The faith in those who went before us—great authorities, Thomas Aquinas, Augustine, to name just a couple. We have been misled.

Another disappointment. A betrayal, even. Another way of feeling abandoned. Unaccompanied. Finally alone.

What is the value of an apocalyptic vision? Certainly, it is a treasure of imagery and imagination. But what kind of behavior does it encourage—or prevent? What kind of God does it suggest? Possibly, it could be a corrective to those who think they can get away with anything. Certainly it plays into our desire for justice. But it is a justice which is inexorably connected with punishment and exclusion.

. . .

RETURNING TO THE JEFFERSONIAN MODEL, I ask myself if I would prefer a Gospel without its apocalyptic sections. Has it been worth the harm that has been done by a self-righteous cohort understanding themselves as an elect, thrilling at the vision of burning others? How do you measure worth?

I know I would miss the thunderous resonance of the words, the art that has been created because of the images. And is there something in the human mind that requires at least some moments of dramatic finality, as a way of assuring us that the end of our lives will not be a nonevent? That part of us that loves the paintings of El Greco, the *Inferno* of Dante, the falling angels of William Blake. I know that when, in the New English Bible, the words "the abomination of desolation" are missing, I throw it down, sniffing in punctilious disgust. Suspecting the airbrush. Suspecting I am being kept from something: The Real thing. The whole story. The door into the terrible. The parts that give our nightmares placement in the light of day.

The apocalyptic takes up only a small back room in the house of my imagination. But people who place it at the center of the house, or think of it as the doorway through which all must enter—these are not my neighbors.

"Who is my neighbor?" Jesus introduces this question in the parable of the Good Samaritan. Perhaps it is a question that can only be answered at the end of time. When there is no more time, what does it matter where you live?

5

Contradiction, Conundrum, Paradox

"You are the light of the world. A city built on a hill cannot be hid. No one after lighting a lamp puts it under a bushel basket, but on the lampstand, and it gives light to all in the house. In the same way, let your light shine before others, so that they may see your good works and give glory to your Father in heaven."

MATTHEW 5:14–16

❧

"Beware of practicing your piety before others in order to be seen by them; for then you have no reward from your Father in heaven.

"So whenever you give alms, do not sound a trumpet before you, as the hypocrites do in the synagogues and in the streets, so that they may be praised by others. Truly I tell you, they have received their reward. But when you give alms, do not let your left hand know what your right hand is doing, so that your alms may be done in secret; and your Father who sees in secret will reward you.

"And whenever you pray, do not be like the hypocrites; for they love to stand and pray in the synagogues and at the street corners, so that they may be seen by others. Truly I tell you, they have received their reward. But whenever you pray, go into your room and shut the door and pray to your Father who is in secret; and your Father who sees in secret will reward you."

MATTHEW 6:1–6

&

Many crowds followed him, and he cured all of them, and he ordered them not to make him known. This was to fulfill what had been spoken through the prophet Isaiah:

"Here is my servant, whom I have chosen,
my beloved, with whom my soul is well pleased.
I will put my spirit upon him,
and he will proclaim justice to the Gentiles.
He will not wrangle or cry aloud,
nor will anyone hear his voice in the streets.
He will not break a bruised reed
or quench a smoldering wick
until he brings justice to victory.
And in his name the Gentiles will hope."

MATTHEW 12:15–21

&

"Do not think that I have come to bring peace to the earth; I have not come to bring peace, but a sword.

146

For I have come to set a man against his father,
and a daughter against her mother,
and a daughter-in-law against her mother-in-law;
and one's foes will be members of one's own household."

MATTHEW 10:34–36

But I say to you, Do not resist an evildoer. But if anyone strikes
you on the right cheek, turn the other also.

MATTHEW 5:39

He said to them, "When I sent you out without a purse, bag, or
sandals, did you lack anything?" They said, "No, not a thing."
He said to them, "But now, the one who has a purse must take it,
and likewise a bag. And the one who has no sword must sell his
cloak and buy one. For I tell you, this scripture must be fulfilled
in me, 'And he was counted among the lawless'; and indeed what
is written about me is being fulfilled." They said, "Lord, look,
here are two swords." He replied, "It is enough."

LUKE 22:35–38

"Put your sword in its scabbard, for all who take the sword will
perish by the sword."   MATTHEW 26:52

"Come to me, all you that are weary and are carrying heavy burdens, and I will give you rest. Take my yoke upon you, and learn from me; for I am gentle and humble in heart, and you will find rest for your souls. For my yoke is easy, and my burden light."

MATTHEW 11:28–30

"Strive to enter through the narrow door; for many, I tell you, will try to enter and will not be able."   LUKE 13:24

"To you has been given the secret of the kingdom of God, but for those outside, everything comes in parables; in order that,

'they may indeed look, but not perceive,
and may indeed listen, but not understand;
so that they may not turn again and be forgiven.'"

MARK 4:11–12

WHEN WE USE THE WORD "LANGUAGE" we do not mean only one thing, and to read as if all words were the same kind of entity and should be read in the same way, to confuse the literal for the metaphoric, is to be classed among the mentally impaired. I once sent an autistic child into a panic by saying, "The heat is killing me." He jumped into his father's arms, screaming, "The lady is dying, the lady is dying!"

But when a certain kind of truth claim has been made for certain words, as it has been for the words of the Bible, how do we know when to read literally and when not to? What is the place of irony, paradox, rhetorical effect, in a text whose synonym is "revelation"? Reveal: to take away the obstacles to comprehension. Conceal: to hide, to create more obstacles. But what is an obstacle and what a challenging and enriching enhancement?

Language is a vehicle of information, but what kind of vehicle is it? We speak to say, "The stove is hot, don't touch it," or, "Get out of the way of the car." There are some sentences that are unequivocal and impermeable to more than one interpretation. But as speaking creatures, we are drawn toward embellishment. Ornamentation, devices. Metaphor—which insists the body partake in the mind's work of comparison. Irony—insisting that we understand that a meaning contains its opposite. But if salvation is at stake, isn't that more like "Get out of the way of the car" than "How sweet the moonlight sleeps upon this bank"? If Jesus really cared about our eternal salvation, shouldn't he have spoken in words as transparent as the Decalogue?

But clearly something important is achieved by more complex rhetorical practices. It seems to me that in the very labor they require, sharper grooves are dug into the surface of the mind. So that understanding is more like transplanting a sapling than snowboarding. You dig down to the depths . . . digging through paradox, metaphor, hyperbole, in order that the thing—the thing one wants to live by—can take root. Probably it is wise to be ready and flexible enough to respond to metaphor. But not always. When Jesus says, "Because she has loved much, much is forgiven her," we want to take him at his word. When he says, "if your eye offends you, pluck it out," we know we'd better not.

Paradoxical language can provide riches of texture, flavor, and a satisfying thickness for the mind's incisors. "Be as wise as serpents and as innocent as doves." Who would quarrel with the literal contradiction? Who would object to that sort of intriguing doubleness? And when Jesus tells his followers to make friends with the mammon of wickedness so that at the end of time they will take you in, we know he's just being ironic to make a point. But if we are taking the words as a prescription for behavior, if one is taking the words of Jesus as a guide to living a virtuous life or even as a species of wisdom literature, the contradictions cease being intellectual puzzles and can become a frustration, a source of outrage or even despair, a reason to turn one's back on Jesus as serious teacher or moral guide.

I ask myself why riddling language seems distressing on Jesus' part, whereas with the Buddha's incomprehensible koans, it's just seen as part of the project. Is it because Jesus suggests that his relationship with us is more personal, that he loves us and we are meant to love him in return? One can admire the incomprehensible; it is hard to love it.

At what point does paradox, which suggests the complexities of life and the demands of understanding, become contradiction, worthy of the accusation we level at a politician—that he's not being consistent, that we don't know what he really stands for, what his values really are, and so he will not get our vote?

Take, for example, the seeming contradictions on the topic of visibility.

In two adjacent chapters, Jesus' words seem to give opposing guidance. In Matthew 5, he tells his followers that they are the light of the world and that they should display their good works. In the following chapter, he counsels them to do everything behind closed doors. So, which is it, the light on the stand or the closed chamber? Certainly, public displays of piety and self-regarding prayer are always obnoxious. But almsgiving might conceivably be of a different order of human act. Isn't it possible to say that a good example might urge others to give alms, and therefore increase the benefit to the poor? Isn't Jesus, in using his candle metaphor, suggesting the positive benefits of display?

But if even your left hand doesn't know what your right hand is doing, how can anyone learn from good example?

In this case, the conundrum is difficult, but not enraging. It is certainly a worthy goal to give for the sake of giving, not for the sake of the praise one gets for the gift. The emphasis, then, is on the gift and the recipient, his or her need in the moment, rather than one's own narcissistic gratification. Certainly, a person of mature ethical thinking understands that in some cases one kind of behavior is called for, and in some it is not. Nevertheless, the closeness of the two passages can be jarring, as if we'd been offered an éclair, complete with descriptions of its delights, and almost immediately lectured on the cleansing benefits of fasting.

. . .

SIMILARLY, JESUS SEEMS TO OFFER contradictory words on the issue of violence. Both proponents of nonviolence and of just war would seem to have justification in his words. The disciples are told to turn the other cheek, and then advised to arm themselves with swords, which they are then told to put in their scabbards. Jesus is fulfilling the Isaian prophecy that the Messiah will not quench a wick, but he is also the one who sets brother against brother. With which, among these excerpts, should we ally ourselves, know ourselves, live by?

These contradictions spread themselves throughout the Gospel narratives, and among the four Evangelists. The passage in which Jesus says he is not bringing peace but the sword occurs in the first third of Matthew; two chapters later is the radically nonviolent passage that recalls the prophecy of Isaiah. The first happens in a series of rather angry instructions to the disciples; the second after he has performed many cures which he understood to have put him in danger with the Pharisees. Neither context offers sufficient explanation for such radically divergent pieces of advice. The passage in Luke in which Jesus (seeming to contradict all his previous advice that comes down against preparedness in opposition to the spontaneity inspired by faith) suggests that now the apostles must be prepared not only with what is needed for their bodily sustenance, but with what aggression requires, occurs at the very end of the Last Supper, just before his entry into the garden, where, in Matthew, he urges his followers not to use the sword. How to reconcile this advice with the words spoken during the Sermon on the Mount, "You have heard that it was said, 'An eye for an eye and a tooth for a tooth.' But I say to you, Do not resist an evildoer. But if anyone strikes you on the right cheek, turn the other also" (Matthew 5:38–39)? And what are we to make of someone who says, "Peace I leave with you," as well as, "I have come not to bring peace, but a sword"?

Of course, one way of coming to terms with this conundrum is to settle on the line that follows—"Peace I leave with you; my peace I give to you"—which occurs during the Last Supper discourse in the Gospel of John. After saying this, Jesus goes on to say, "I do not give to you as the world gives." This is a position which people of faith fall back on, to the outrage of people who reject this way of seeing. It is the default position of mystery: there are things out there, Horatio, beyond our understanding. But what if, for example, one were trying to make a decision whether or not to be a conscientious objector, believing in Jesus as, if not divine, a supreme ethical guide? Which passages of the Gospel would you turn to, bearing in mind that your own life and the lives of strangers (also children of God) are at stake? In such a situation, is Jesus a help or a source of frustration? In what way is he a guide? And what path is he indicating, and what would the nature of following be?

A related question: How does one follow, and what is required of a follower? Once again, Jesus seems to offer conflicting models: the yoke that is sweet, the burden that is light, and the narrow gate that many will not get through. Which of these are we meant to understand when we try to make sense of our relationship with Jesus and his father, what that might feel like, who we think we are in relationship with, and what that relationship requires?

If we imagine a physical or somatic encounter with the human Jesus inspired by these passages—the light burden, the narrow gate—the pictures we would come up with are quite different. One would suggest a relaxed embrace, a supple spine, eyes half closed, lips relaxed into a trusting smile. The other would require an alert vigilance: a straight spine, a self-regarding, self-questioning anxiety, a fear of approaching the exigent gatekeeper, for whom trying is not enough, not even perhaps trying one's best.

I looked up each of these passages using Google, and the results were fascinating, if not surprising. The "narrow gate" passage was invoked punitively and to indicate the superiority and exclusive claim of Christianity. It was often used politically, particularly in opposition to abortion rights. The "light burden" passage was much more emotional and psychological; ethical terms were not invoked. Both had media accompaniments. One site, which belonged to traditional Catholics, included a kind of image familiar to my fifties childhood: a priest with his back to the congregation elevating the host high above his and their heads; the musical accompaniment was the Latin hymn "O Salutaris Hostia"; a second had a background of a rising sun, and provided a visual link to the hymn "What a friend we have in Jesus" to the accompaniment of a harmonium. Another link is to Bobby K, who offers "a cool jazzy rendition that beckons the hearer to a more spiritual life." He describes his music as "music with a healing, uplifting and inspiring message to mend hurting and broken lives and bring encouragement to people in all walks of their faith."

Is it enough for the Gospels to be a prototype for twelve-step programs? On the other hand, of what use is the impulse to exclusion and anxiety?

It is no surprise that the same Jesus was worshipped by Jonathan Edwards and Julian of Norwich, one of whom tells us that we are sinners in the hands of an angry God, and the other who assures us, "All shall be well, and shall be well, and all manner of things shall be well."

WHAT IS THE PLACE OF the incomprehensible in a text if we understand that it is meant to serve as our guide not only to a good life but to something called salvation? Shouldn't such a text refuse the obfuscation that occurs from contradiction, shouldn't it yield up, after careful study, a transparency? But how is transparency possible if contradictions serve, rather than as transparent glass, as veils whose thickness obscures the light? What to do with the passages that seem to give the lie to everything that has been said before? There is always the "it was a mistranslation . . . something was left out that would make sense of it" argument. But the fact is, this is the text we have. The text that was deliberately selected and ferociously preserved. Something was at stake in including these sections, or in not taking them out. And what was that thing at stake? And for whom?

One example of incomprehensibility that is numinous rather than confounding is the incident of the naked young man in the garden of Mark's Gospel. It seems random, odd, tantalizingly elusive, but, having no ethical or epistemic content, it does nothing to shake anyone's faith.

But how are we to understand these words from Luke, "From those who have little, even the little they have will be taken away" (Luke 8:18–19)—as a moment of almost nihilistic despair at the fate of the poor? Or, connected as it would seem to be tonally to Matthew's parable of the talents, is there any surprise that it should be read, as certain Calvinists did, as a blueprint to justify any excess of laissez-faire capitalism: the poor are poor because God wants them to be? In this story, the master gives to one of his servants ten talents (a talent was a monetary unit, not just a metaphor); to another, five; to the third, one. The lucky two invest theirs and make profits; the third, fearful, buries his and so earns no interest at all. He explains his behavior in this way: "Master, I knew that you were a harsh man, reaping where you did not sow, and gathering where you did not scatter seed; so I was afraid, and I went and hid your talent in the ground. Here you have what is yours."

The master is without compassion for what would seem to be the servant's entirely justified fear. The poor servant doesn't even get credit for returning his master's initial investment. Rather, he is greeted with rage, with the very harshness that the servant understood to be his dominant characteristic:

"You wicked and lazy slave! You knew, did you, that I reap where I did not sow, and gather where I did not scatter? Then you ought to have invested my money with the bankers, and on my return I would have received what was my own with interest. So take the talent from him, and give it to the one with the ten talents. For to all those who have, more will be given, and they will have an abundance, but from those who have nothing, even what they have will be taken away. As for this worthless slave, throw him into the outer darkness, where there will be weeping and gnashing of teeth." MATTHEW 25:24–30

The passage is even more problematic because it immediately precedes the section in which Jesus insists that those who have refused to give food, drink, and clothing to the poor—because they didn't notice them, didn't realize that they were Jesus—will be condemned to everlasting fire. It would seem that the fearful, meagerly gifted servant is the same as the careless prosperous ones who pass the starving poor without a second glance. Is the parable simply a rather cynical interpretation of the phenomenon of bad luck? Or are we to understand God as not only harsh, but irrationally so? How, then, could we confidently address him as Father? Why would we not believe that if we asked him for a fish he would respond with a scorpion?

. . .

EVEN MORE PROBLEMATIC is Jesus' explanation of the parable of
the sower in Mark 4. The chapter begins with Jesus' telling of the
sower who sowed some seed on the path, where it was eaten by birds;
some on rocky ground, where it sprang up quickly and withered
quickly; some among thorns, where it was choked; and some on good
soil.

It would seem that the parable is the opposite of difficult; no especially gifted interpreter is required to shed his hermeneutical light.
The problem occurs when the disciples (not noted for their quickness
of wit or understanding) ask Jesus for help. He says to them, "To you
has been given the secret of the kingdom of God, but for those outside, everything comes in parables; in order that 'they may indeed
look, but not perceive, and may indeed listen, but not understand; so
that they may not turn again and be forgiven.'"

Frank Kermode turns his full critical attention to this passage in
his masterly study *The Genesis of Secrecy*. He cites it as a problem connected with the very enterprise of interpretation, which suggests that
there are insiders and outsiders, those who are allowed to understand,
or who are given the right tools for comprehension, and those who are
not. He notes that these words of Jesus echo Isaiah 6:9–10:

"Go and say to this people: 'Keep listening, but do not
comprehend; keep looking, but do not understand.' Make
the mind of this people dull, and stop their ears, and shut
their eyes, so that they may not look with their eyes, and
listen with their ears, and comprehend with their minds,
and turn and be healed." Then I said, "How long, O
Lord?" And he said: "Until cities lie waste without

inhabitant, and houses without people, and the land is utterly desolate; until the Lord sends everyone far away, and vast is the emptiness in the midst of the land. Even if a tenth part remain in it, it will be burned again, like a terebinth or an oak whose stump remains standing when it is felled." The holy seed is its stump.

The notion of holy speech whose intention is to mislead, deceive, or exclude—God says this to Isaiah after the angel cleanses his lips with the burning coal, thereby readying them for pure words—is difficult enough to come to terms with in Yahweh, whom we expect to be punitive toward his people. But in Jesus, who is "meek and humble of heart," who will "take all people to himself"—it becomes incomprehensible or, in the words of Albert Schweitzer, "repellent."

Kermode gives a thorough account of the scholarly debates about this Markan passage, focusing on the word *hina*, "in order that." In Mark, Jesus says he speaks in parables in order that people might not understand, whereas in Matthew, Jesus uses the word *hoti*, "because" they do not understand. Some scholars feel that *hina* was a mistranscription. Nonetheless it is an error that the compilers of the Gospels retained, and the question is: Why?

Certainly, it provides a justification for a priesthood of interpretation. But what can, and indeed has, resulted from this Gospel passage can seem to have been a malign outcome, particularly considering Jesus' repeated interdictions against hierarchical power grabbing, and his preference for the poor and the uneducated. But even if the passage is interpreted as a justification for a sorely needed institutional church, Jesus' impulse purposely to confound—in order that some might not repent and be saved—seems at best adolescently churlish, at worst punitively sadistic. It is an impulse reminiscent of Jonah's hope that the Ninevites won't repent and he can laugh at their destruction—an impulse that God punishes and marks as wrong. How do we explain this in the Lamb of God, who takes away the sins of the world, who draws everyone to himself?

And how do the Gospels taken as a whole suggest that the reader shape a relationship with God? In fear or in trust? Who is he? And who is Jesus? And how do we forgive him for giving us such mixed messages about what is required of us, how hopeless or hopeful, how confident or terrified we should be? Of what use are the Gospels in helping us to live not just a good life, but any kind of coherent life at all? Or do they condemn us to a maddening dance on a constantly shifting, constantly unstable ground, a life of vertigo, a wounded, baffled envy of those who can take their place on the firm dry soil of rational unbelief?

6

The Tainted Text:
The Problem
of the Jews

"Many will come from east and west and will eat with Abraham and Isaac and Jacob in the kingdom of heaven, while the heirs of the kingdom will be thrown into the outer darkness, where there will be weeping and gnashing of teeth." MATTHEW 8:11–12

Jesus said to them, "Have you never read in the scriptures:

'The stone that the builders rejected has become the cornerstone . . . '

Therefore I tell you, the kingdom of God will be taken away from you and given to a people that produces the fruits of the kingdom. The one who falls on this stone will be broken to pieces; and it will crush anyone on whom it falls." MATTHEW 21:42–44

Then Jesus said to the Jews who had believed in him, "If you continue in my word, you are truly my disciples; and you will know the truth, and the truth will make you free." They answered him, "We are descendents of Abraham and have never been slaves to anyone. What do you mean by saying, 'You will be made free?'"

Jesus answered them, "Very truly, I tell you, everyone who commits sin is a slave to sin. The slave does not have a permanent place in the household; the son has a place there forever. So if the Son makes you free, you will be free indeed. I know that you are descendents of Abraham; yet you look for an opportunity to kill me, because there is no place in you for my word" . . .

They answered him, "Abraham is our father." Jesus said to them, "If you were Abraham's children, you would be doing what Abraham did, but now you are trying to kill me, a man who has told you the truth that I heard from God. This is not what Abraham did. You are indeed doing what your father does." They said to him, "We are not illegitimate children; we have one father, God himself." Jesus said to them, "If God were your Father, you would love me, for I came from God and now I am here. I did not come on my own, but he sent me. Why do you not understand what I say? It is because you cannot accept my word. You are from your father the devil, and you choose to do your father's desires. He was a murderer from the beginning and does not stand in the truth, because there is no truth in him. When he lies, he speaks according to his own nature, for he is a liar and the father of lies. But because I tell the truth, you do not believe me. Which of you convicts me of sin? If I tell the truth, why do you not believe me? Whoever is from God hears the words of God. The reason you do not hear them is that you are not from God."

The Jews answered him, "Are we not right in saying that you are a Samaritan and have a demon?" Jesus answered, "I do not have a demon; but I honor my Father, and you dishonor me. Yet I do not seek my own glory; there is one who seeks it and he is the judge. Very truly, I tell you, whoever keeps my word will never see death." The Jews said to him, "Now we know that you have a demon. Abraham died, and so did the prophets; yet you say, 'Whoever keeps my word will never taste death.' Are you greater than our father Abraham, who died? The prophets also died. Who do you claim to be?" Jesus answered, "If I glorify myself, my glory is nothing. It is my Father who glorifies me, he of whom you say, 'He is our God,' though you do not know him. But I know him; if I would say that I do not know him, I would be a liar like you. But I do know him and I keep his word. Your ancestor Abraham rejoiced that he would see my day; he saw it and was glad." Then the Jews said to him, "You are not yet fifty years old, and have you seen Abraham?" Jesus said to them, "Very truly, I tell you, before Abraham was, I am." So they picked up stones to throw at him, but Jesus hid himself and went out of the temple.   JOHN 8:31–59

❦

While they were going, some of the guard went into the city and told the chief priest everything that had happened. After the priests had assembled with the elders, they devised a plan to give a large sum of money to the soldiers, telling them, "You must say, 'His disciples came by night and stole him away while we were asleep.' If this comes to the governor's ears, we will satisfy him and keep you out of trouble." So they took the money and did as they were directed. And this story is still told among the Jews to this day. MATTHEW 28:11–15

§

When Pilate saw that he could do nothing, but rather that a riot was beginning, he took some water and washed his hands before the crowd, saying, "I am innocent of this man's blood; see to it yourselves." Then the people as a whole answered, "His blood be upon us and our children." MATTHEW 27:24–25

IT WOULD BE HARD to find words written at any point in history as drenched in blood as these. From the persecutors of Jews in the Middle Ages to the Inquisitors to Hitler's troops to blogging neo-Nazis, the words of the Gospels have been used to justify the murder of Jews. I have read these words, I have written them by hand in my notebook, the notebook headed "Jesus," and then I have typed them on my computer screen. Each time, I hope that they will be different, that they weren't as bad as I thought. That the imagery is not so violent; that I will not find words like "crushed," "outer darkness," "your father the devil," "his blood be on our heads." These passages stifle my impulse to interpretation, as if the very act of interpretation were a refusal to face the horror, like defending a mass murderer on the grounds that he grew up in difficult circumstances, or that he has a fine tenor voice.

I did, however, find myself tempted to a literary interpretation of one passage, the one in which the Jews call Jesus' blood upon my head. Reading it, I see that it's possible to think of it as an example of dramatic irony. We know that Jesus' blood is upon everyone . . . the precious blood—doesn't this make the Jews more specially favored in the sight of God because of their ironic, unknowing request? But such an interpretation would be of interest only to someone who began by desiring such an interpretation; it could never undo the impulse to murderous violence . . . you can't stop a rhinoceros with a feather. And so I stop myself; the exercise seems to me an exercise in mandarin impiety. I prefer shocked silence.

This impulse—the impulse to shocked silence—may be a self-protective gesture, and it is one rejected by the scholars who have devoted themselves to the project of contextualizing John's anti-

Jewishness. Because of their work, we must now see the Gospel placed in the context of the Johannine community, which had just been expelled from the synagogue in the late first century. Unfortunately, the cool rationality of contextualization doesn't neutralize the hateful poison of the words, repeated, and heated up after centuries of repetition, fueled by the energy of centuries of shouting vengeful mobs.

I CAN HEAR ALL TOO CLEARLY the roar of those mobs, and hearing it, I hear as well the cry of insistence: the voice of the Just Witness, demanding that I abandon the Gospels as the work of bloody-minded men recording the words of a bloody-minded leader. Hearing this voice, I experience shame in relation to my own Jewishness, my Jewish father and forebears, my beloved Jewish friends, above all the victims of Jewish hatred throughout the ages. In the interest of justice, in the interest of witness, should I amputate my attachment to the Gospels? Is anything worth the taking of all these innocent lives?

What would the implications of such an amputation be? How would one name, or limn the loss? If I reject the Gospel of Matthew, I lose the Beatitudes, Jesus' ethical insistence that the duty to needy human beings is located in his person, his own flesh . . . and necessarily Bach's *St. Matthew Passion,* my favorite music. If I refuse John, I refuse what the Johannine scholar Sandra Schneiders thinks of as the Johannine trinity, the Gospel of love, life, and light.* I lose "In the Beginning was the word," the image of the Lamb of God, the living water, Jesus as light, the story of the Samaritan woman, the wedding at Cana, the woman taken in adultery, the blind man whose restora-

---

* Sandra M. Schneiders, *Written That You May Believe* (New York: Crossroad, 1999), p. 52.

tion of sight makes the point that afflicted children have not been punished for their own sins or the sins of their parents. I lose the sentence that has been a crucial source of my faith: "I have come that you may have life and have it more abundantly." What kind of scale can be used to measure the beauty, the inspiration that these words have provided, against the weight of the bodies of the millions of dead whose destruction they have justified?

Even a Jeffersonian bowdlerization would not suffice; it might change a future reading, but it could not erase the harm that has gone before. Are these words like Walter Benjamin's angel of history, blown back in time, a filthy and murderous wind that cannot be cleansed, whose destruction cannot be undone?

I cannot find a place to stand on this question that is not, for me, a place of torment. I understand that the torment is not something I have invented, something I experience without accompaniment. Since the Shoah proved the scope and range of hatred of Jews, Christian scholars of goodwill have tried to make sense of the problem of anti-Jewishness in the Gospels. Scholars of distinction have devoted themselves to examination of the problem—a problem that is named sometimes as a hermeneutical challenge, a linguistic task, a work of historicization, and sometimes included in all these approaches, a cry of outraged, grieving witness.

Among the most outstanding of these scholars was Raymond Brown, a lover of John's Gospel who presented the terms, with his customary rigor, in unflinching plainness:

It would be incredible for a twentieth-century Christian to share or justify the Johannine contention that "the Jews" are the children of the devil, an affirmation which is placed on the lips of

Jesus; but I cannot see how it helps contemporary Jewish-
Christian relationships to disguise the fact that such an attitude
once existed.

Brown won't buy the argument that "the Jews" should be read as "only
some of the Jews." He quotes a Johannine scholar, John Ashton, in
saying, "It is not just the Pharisees that attract his [the Evangelist's] ire
and resentment; it is the Jewish people as a whole who are made the
symbol of the human shadow."* He continues with the observation:

Uncomfortable as that may make modern readers because of the
horrible history of anti-Jewish persecution in subsequent histories, it is what John meant. If he describes "the Jews" as wanting
to put Jesus to death, he has Jesus predict that the synagogue
Jews will put his followers to death. The Gospel portrayal has
been colored by Johannine dualism where there is only light and
darkness, truth and falsehood, so that opponents are painted as
blind and false. Kysar contends that while the Gospel is not
anti-Jewish, it can nurture anti-Judaism. Cook . . . is uncomfort-
ably correct in pointing out that John may give the impression
that God is anti-Jewish. Today, therefore, in proclaiming John
preachers must be careful to caution hearers that John's passages
cannot be used to justify any ongoing hostility to Jewish people,
any more than one should appeal for justification in our times to
the genocidal cleansings of Palestine described in the Old Testament as God's instruction for Israel at the time of Joshua's con-

---

* Raymond E. Brown, *The Community of the Beloved Disciple* (New York: Paulist Press, 1979),
p. 41.

quest. Regarding the bible as sacred does not mean that everything described therein is laudable.*

But interpretation is dependent upon the interpreter, as James D.
G. Dunn notes in his essay "The Embarrassment of History: Reflec-
tions on the Problem of Anti-Judaism in the Fourth Gospel":

> The issue came home to me some years ago, when, after a week
> in which I had been reflecting on the question of anti-Semitism
> in the New Testament, I heard a sermon in Durham Cathedral
> in which John 8 (The Gospel reading for the day) was
> expounded straightforwardly as denouncing the Jews and
> Judaism, with little or no qualification.†

It is impossible to guard against the biased or unintelligent homilist;
or to provide everyone who owns a Bible with responsible scholarly
commentary.

This problem of the history of interpretation was discussed in
2000, in an interdisciplinary seminar held at the University of Leuven
specifically to study the problem of anti-Jewishness in the Gospel of
John. Twenty-four scholars, in both the fields of Johannine studies
and Jewish-Christian relations, met to consider this grave issue. The
proceedings of the seminar were published in a book called *Anti-
Judaism and the Fourth Gospel*. I find these words in the introduction to
this volume, and I am moved by their nuanced yet unflinching facing

---

* Raymond E. Brown, *An Introduction to the Gospel of John* (New York: Anchor Bible, 2003),
p. 93.
† R. Bieringer, D. Pollefeyt, and F. Vandecasteele-Vanneuville, eds., *Anti-Judaism and the
Fourth Gospel* (Louisville, KY: Westminster John Knox Press, 2001), p. 41.

of the problem, a testimony to the labor of honest intellectual confrontation—a sign of the only hope possible: that such words may be more widely accessible, spoken not only in seminars, but in pulpits and church basements.

They reject the tempting way out: that the problem lies not in the Gospel itself but in the history of its interpretation. They ask:

Does not the history of interpretation become part of the meaning of the text itself? Has the text not lost its innocence and become guilty? Moreover, while an individual "critic" might indeed misjudge the meaning of the text, it is much more difficult to defend that the mainstream in Christian tradition has created its anti-Jewish interpretations from nothing.*

As a way of understanding their problem, what to do with the Gospel of John, the authors of the introduction examine the case of the Catholic cathedral of Brussels. It has magnificent stained-glass windows from the sixteenth to the nineteenth century, the subject of which is the legend of host-profanation. In 1370, some Jews in Brussels were accused of stealing hosts and piercing them with knives. The hosts began to bleed. The cathedral became a locus of pious devotion to the miracle of the bleeding hosts.

The authors ask, what is to be done with these windows? They offer three possibilities. The first would be to remove the windows, along with every evidence of anti-Judaism that is a part of European cultural history. Another option would be to provide information so

---

* R. Bieringer, D. Pollefeyt, and F. Vandecasteele-Vanneuville, eds., *Anti-Judaism and the Fourth Gospel* (Louisville, KY: Westminster John Knox Press, 2001), p.7.

that the historical background of the windows is made clear. A third would be to hope that the heinousness of what is depicted would be so obvious that nothing need be done about it. In the end, the leadership of the archdiocese of Malines-Brussels chose to draw attention to the legendary nature of the "miracle" by putting up a bronze plate with the following text: "In 1968, in the spirit of the Second Vatican Council, and taking note of historical research, the leadership of the diocese of Malines-Brussels has drawn . . . attention to the biased nature of the accusation and the legendary character of the 'miracle.'"

One asks oneself: In what language were the words on the plaque written? What size was it? How visible was it? Did it interfere with the architecture of the cathedral, renowned for its beauty? How many people saw it . . . and was it too little too late?

Would it be possible to have a fourth option, not to remove the windows but, as a public act of repentance for its use as a site which reenacted anti-Semitism, to deconsecrate the cathedral, name it no longer a sacred space?

Would it be possible to deconsecrate the Gospels? To complicate the meaning of revelation to include the revelation of its own potential for harm?

What would that mean?

It would mean to read these words as if they were written by fallible human beings, capable, therefore, of gross errors and grotesque misdirections. Do these errors and misdirections remove them from the possibility of the holy?

But whatever angle we approach the Gospels from, their treatment of the Jews must confront us with a spectacle of horror. We can begin with Raymond Brown's perceptive "Regarding the bible as sacred does not mean that everything described therein is laudable." But we must go further. What if the texts are not only unlaudable, but wicked?

Then we must face the larger question: How much blood needs to be shed in the name of a sacred text before we can no longer call it sacred? Or are only parts of it sacred? And then, which parts?

What happens if we must think of the sacred as partial?

The sacred as broken?

Unwhole.

READING THE DECONSECRATED text would be to understand that, in loving it, we turn the pages leaving behind us bloody fingerprints, the blood of murdered Jews seeping into the lines that make up our individual fingerprints, our individual responses to these words, the individual ways we have taken them into our lives. The pages are stained with blood. We cannot read them purely. We cannot read them innocently. They must be read supported by an undertone of lamentation. We must always read these words with a broken heart.

7

The Problem
of Divinity

"Very truly, I tell you, before Abraham was, I am."

JOHN 8:58

I HAVE AN IRISH FRIEND who is the person I have known best who most closely embodies the holy, although he would hate to hear me saying that. I ask him if he thinks Jesus is God. "I do," he says, "only I'm not quite sure what God is."

Many people would say that it is not possible to call oneself a Christian and not to assert that Jesus is God. But like my friend, I don't know quite what I mean when I say the word "God."

And what does it mean to say that someone is God who has been historically verified to have lived on earth in a human form? And on what grounds would one either affirm or deny the Incarnation—the idea that in Jesus God became man? Is there anything in a text that could justify such an assertion, an assertion which logically seems impossible?

Most of the terms that Jesus uses for himself, or that are used about him, "Messiah," "Son of God," "Son of Man," were used in Scripture for others: David, Daniel, Elijah—and don't necessarily insist upon divinity. Even the beginning of John—"In the beginning was the Word, and the Word was with God, and the Word was God. He was in the beginning with God"—doesn't require belief in a uniquely divine nature. Later, in the words that give shape to the idea of the Incarnation, "And the Word became flesh and lived among us, and we have seen his glory, the glory as of a father's only son," an important inclusion is the words "as of."

In the problematic section of John in which Jesus suggests that the devil is the father of the Jews, he says, "Before Abraham was, I am," which makes the claim, if not for divinity, then for a being and existence outside time. And the use of the words "I am," echoes Yahweh's self-definition in the burning bush. If we choose not to believe these words literally, what do we do with them? Fob them off on authorial agenda ... or say we don't really understand time, that time, all of our time on earth, what we call a lifetime, is larger and stranger than what we thought? Neither of these satisfies me, or lets me off the hook of the responsibility to ask the question: Is Jesus divine? I was thinking for a moment that it would be wonderful if someone said that John 8 didn't really make the canonical text—but then I would have to lose the story of the woman taken in adultery. Ironically, it is this story that scholars are willing to name as possibly suspect, not the anti-Semitic portions or the assertion of Jesus' existence outside time. And here we see the pain and paradox of reading the Gospels.

Before reading the Gospels, during our reading, and after it, a question hovers above the enterprise: What is at stake in the assertion that Jesus is God?

The malign implications in the belief that Jesus is, unique among all humans who have lived, divine, are clear. It necessitates the belief in the superiority, or the exclusive truth content, of Christianity. If Jesus is God, all those who deny or can't see it have missed something enormous in the universe: if one believes the earth is round, it is false to say that people who think it's flat have just as good a claim on truth. If you asked me, though, why I believe the earth is round, I can't tell you ... only that a lot of people seem to say it is, and some people can understand the proofs. That I can't, that that kind of mathematical or spatial understanding is beyond me, doesn't cause me to be tolerant of flat-earthers. On the other hand, not much is affected by my belief that the earth is round. I wouldn't live differently if I thought it were flat. I would not understand my place on the flat or round earth differently, I would not treat my fellow humans differently, I would be neither more nor less despairing, more nor less confident. But I would feel contemptuous of those who held on to an older, or different, conception of the shape of the earth.

So does belief in the divinity of Jesus necessitate creedal superiority? Only, I think, if one oversimplifies the question, and that is why I think reading the Gospels (as opposed to the Epistles) opens and complicates it—in ways that must be good.

It is because the Gospels are narrative that their flexibility and porosity is inherent. There is no such thing as one narrative. We are, as a species, narrative-makers; we seem to need that particular habit . . . the habit of having moving and speaking creatures follow a set of events that are connected and result in an outcome. We do it and do it, and the narratives are impressed by our culture, our histories, our accidents in time. The narrative of the Gospels has been extraordinarily compelling for millions of people for a couple of thousands of years. But does that mean it's the only story? That would seem to me impossible.

My first experience of doubt happened when I was ten years old. I was very worried about the Chinese, who were living under godless Communism . . . so many millions of them, for whom the word "teeming" seemed to have been invented. But one of my worries about them—beside the fact that I was afraid they would take over the world—was that they were all going to be deprived of heaven. I particularly concentrated on girls of my age, whom I saw as very serious, very bookish, each with a single long pigtail. I thought that some of them could be my friends. This anxiety was connected to my belief that without baptism, one would have, at best, an eternity of limbo, which always seemed a gray and, worse, a boring place—until it was abolished, but by then I was in my teens and it was too late for me, and the Chinese. But at ten, I said to a priest, "How can God not allow good people into heaven if they lived in a place and time when they could never have heard of Jesus?" To his credit, the priest went silent. Of responses, this was not the worst. But it didn't take away my doubts.

What is lost if we give up the idea that Jesus is God incarnate? It is an idea I find myself, oddly, unwilling to give up. Because the incarnate God is a potent embodiment of what I think of as the truth about the human lot: that we are mixed, flesh, blood, spirit, mind—and that the holy is inseparable, not only from matter, but from the narrative of our lives. It is certainly the case that most religious traditions are involved in the project of making the ordinary holy. But the example of Jesus makes the project biographical. If the experience of birth, friendship, suffering, and death was shared by the divine, a relationship of intimacy, and a refusal of dualism, is necessitated. And this, to me, is a pearl of great price.

What I don't think is justified in the Gospels is the notion that only Jesus was divine, the insistence that God—whoever he or she is—has or can inhabit a human life only once.

The possibility that Jesus is divine comes to me from his story, its varied richness, its enduring power. I can see that the weight of such a claim might seem ridiculously light. But how would one prove or disprove divinity on the basis of a written text? Against what words could the truth value of such a claim be measured? And what difference would such a claim make to the way one lived a life?

8

Wrestling

IN HER MAGNIFICENT *Texts of Terror,* the Biblical scholar Phyllis Trible invokes the image of Jacob wrestling with the angel as a way of understanding how to deal with painful Biblical texts, in particular stories that point to the oppression of women:

> As a paradigm for encountering terror, this story offers suste-
> nance. . . . To tell and hear tales of terror is to wrestle demons in
> the night, without a compassionate God to save us. In combat
> we wonder about the names of the demons. Our own names,
> however, we all too frightfully recognize. But yet we hold on,
> seeking a blessing: the healing of wounds and the restoration
> of health. If the blessing comes—and we dare not claim
> assurance—it does not come on our terms. Indeed, as we leave
> the land of terror, we limp.*

If I would not go so far as to say that I have, in writing about the problem of Jesus, inhabited the land of terror, I have certainly inhab-ited the land of loss. Anger has been my companion. Disappoint-

---

* Phyllis Trible, *Texts of Terror* (Philadelphia: Fortress Press, 1984), pp. 4–5.

ment. A sense of abandonment. A sense of shame. The God of love has uttered words that make it impossible for me to love him.

"Reading," "love" . . . how do the two words connect? What other reading would threaten love? Love letters, turned to letters of accusation and abandonment, perhaps, but those are private and there have never been words more public than the words of the Gospel. If a writer earned my love by something he wrote, could he lose it by something else? I can't think of an example. I love T. S. Eliot and his anti-Semitism has disappointed me, but I don't love him in a way that constitutes or threatens my identity; I can demote him and replace him with, say, Elizabeth Bishop with no major upending of the epistemic apple cart. I could, I suppose, replace Jesus with Yahweh, Allah, or Krishna, or the Buddha, or Nature or Art. But not without ripping out the foundations of who I am, how I have known myself and understood the world.

Jesus has demanded my love, he has assured me that he loves me, and yet he has said words which are, in Trible's terms, if not terrifying, then terrible.

It would be entirely understandable to renounce my citizenship in this country of disappointed love. Many of my elders and betters have done so.

What am I waiting for?

What are the words that would tip the balance, one way or another, in favor of belief or unbelief? That would allow me to say which matters more, the mysterious vision of an impossible love, or the impossible combination of words that are spoken in the name of death?

Who has the last word, and what might that word be?

III

The Seven
Last Words and
the Last Words

"Eli, Eli, lama sabachthani? . . . My God, my God, why hast thou forsaken me?" MATTHEW 27:46

"Father, forgive them; for they know not what they do."

LUKE 24:34

"This day thou shalt be with me in paradise." LUKE 24:43

"Into thy hands I commend my spirit." LUKE 24:46

"Woman, behold thy son, son behold thy mother."

JOHN 19:26–27

"I thirst." JOHN 19:28

"It is finished." JOHN 19:30

"Who are you looking for?"
She thought it was the gardener.
"Don't touch me."

JOHN 20:15–16

HERE ARE TWO RESPONSES to the death of Jesus on the cross. They are both from Jews, neither a believer. One, an American, is a concert pianist with an enviable career and a reputation for playing the great repertoire of the eighteenth and nineteenth centuries. The other, a refugee from Hitler's Germany, is a successful businessman, a collector of beautiful objects who was taught tennis in 1920s Berlin by a young Russian named Vladimir Nabokov.

When speaking of the death of Jesus, the pianist became irate. The idea that God would demand the death of his son was to him hateful. For him such a suggestion was one of the things that made the idea of God untenable; even if such a God existed, he could not be a God of love; therefore, if he elicited any response it would be one not of love but at best a rebellious contempt.

Nabokov's tennis student said, "The cross is the greatest symbol the human race has been able to come up with."

Here is a third response, from a visual artist, also an unbeliever, who habitually creates crosses out of copper and other metals: He becomes furious when these images are placed in a church. He insists that the cross is of interest to him only formally.

How are we to read the Passion and death of Jesus? What are we to do with it, how are we to place it in the prose work that is the Gospels? It is not the end of the story, but it is the point of highest drama.

Is it possible to read the Passion banishing the words "redemption" and "salvation"? Is it possible to experience it as it follows upon other events presented by the Gospel writers? The answer, of course, is no, it is never possible to read these words in the comparatively clear light of literary endeavor. But if, for a moment, we would only follow the words, what would we find?

BECAUSE OF THE WAY these words have come to be known by us—they have been heard probably more than they have been read, and they cannot be heard or read cut off from history or from the pressures they have put upon our lives—our first inclination is to run the various parts of the story together. But what would happen if they were, for a moment, separated, set apart? If our most important unit were the moment?

If we focus on the moment as moment, we are committed to a radical present. We inhabit the terrain of experience rather than implication. If we allow the experience of an experience; if we defer interpretation, allowing the events themselves to wash over and then penetrate us—what kinds of comprehensions might then follow?

And what happens if we read these sentences as sentences, as images, as artifacts made of words? What would happen if we decontextualized sentences, phrases, images, unseated them from their narrative context, framed them with silence, surrounded them with emptiness so that they stand out as singularities against a background of sheer darkness, or silence, like the figures in a Caravaggio or a Fra Angelico, where the lucidity is intensely marked because of the emptiness from which it emanates? A different kind of attention would be required if we were to surround these moments with an emptiness that would allow them to be most singularly themselves.

IF WE LOOKED ON these sentences as sentences, we would be struck by the extraordinary range of diction and literary strategies that happen in these pages. It is surprising to note how few pages they are. In the Revised Standard edition, Matthew's Passion story takes up five pages; Mark's runs less than four, as does Luke's. Even John, the most prolix, requires only ten.

In these pages can be found some of the most important images in the mind of the West, and in the individual lives of centuries of believers. The density of the narrative is enriched and darkened by the power of the images in which they nest:

And when they came to a place called Golgotha (which means Place of a Skull) they offered him wine to drink mixed with gall, but when he tasted it he would not drink it.

From noon on, darkness came over the whole land until three in the afternoon.

A certain young man was following him, wearing nothing but a linen cloth. They caught hold of him but he left the linen cloth and ran off naked.

And he broke down and wept.

"For the days are surely coming when they will say, 'Blessed are the barren and the wombs that never bore, and the breasts that never nursed.' Then they will begin to say to the mountains, 'Fall on us,' and to the hills, 'Cover us.' For if they do this when the wood is green, what will happen when it is dry?"

After receiving the piece of bread he immediately went out.

And it was night.

One of the first things we might notice is the physical power of the images. The power of these images is part and parcel of the power of the Passion: it is rooted in the body, the body of the innocent beloved.

But alongside these intensely vivid images, we find in the pages of the Passion the language of ideas. Luke's language is more abstract than Matthew's and Mark's, and, predictably, John's Gospel is more marked than any of the others by the language of ideas.

The Jesus whom we encounter in Luke and John hurls both ethical and ontological assertions at the apostles even as he is readying himself for his own death. Particularly in John's Passion narrative, Jesus throws these ideas at the disciples with an almost desperate velocity— the teacher who knows this is his last lecture, the term is over, there will be no more time to give the students what he knows. It is almost jarring to experience the alternation of narrative detail and theological idea. Immediately after the dramatic declarative "And it was night," which follows Judas' leave-taking, Jesus says, "I give you a new commandment, that you love one another. Just as I have loved you, you also should love one another. By this everyone will know that you are my disciples, if you have love for one another." Having predicted Peter's denial he then says, "I am the way, and the truth, and the life. No one comes to the Father except through me. If you know me, you will know my Father also." This introduces a discourse on Jesus' relationship to the father, his identification with the father. In the next paragraph, after assuring the apostles, "I will not leave you orphaned," he repeats the word "love" seven times, and the importance of love is stated in the clearest possible terms: "This is my commandment, that you love one another as I have loved you. No one has greater love than this, to lay down one's life for one's friends."

He promises peace, but complicates the promise: "I do not give to you as the world gives." He names himself as the vine: "I am the vine, you are the branches. Those who abide in me and I in them bear much fruit."

ABOVE ALL, THOUGH, the Passion is a history of events. And if we focus on the narrative differences among the four Evangelists, we encounter not only the tonal differences among the writers of the Gospels that mark the entire work, but a difference in emphasis. But for many of us, having heard in church, on the successive days of Holy Week, each of the versions, our experience of the Passion is a composite: for many of us, it is impossible to say which detail comes from which writer. I was surprised to learn that some important moments occur in only one of the Gospels. I had always assumed that the event of the healing of the cut-off ear of Malchus was common to every account. The event occurs in the garden when Jesus is about to be arrested. One of the disciples cuts off the ear of the servant of the high priest. Each Gospel mentions that a disciple (Peter or another) cut off the ear—a striking example of bad strategizing and inexplicably poor impulse control. But only Luke has the servant healed, just as he is the only one to include the puzzling moment when Jesus tells the apostles to take two swords:

> "Now, the one who has a purse must take it, and likewise a bag. And the one who has no sword must sell his cloak and buy one. For I tell you, this scripture must be fulfilled in me, 'And he was counted among the lawless,' and indeed what is written about me is being fulfilled." They said, "Lord, look, here are two swords." He replied, "It is enough."   LUKE 22:35-39

Matthew, Mark, and Luke place the washing of Jesus' feet by

Mary just before Judas' betrayal, perhaps as the motivation for it. For Luke, the washing of the feet occurs much earlier, in chapter 8.

And only Mark includes the strange incident of the naked young man running into the darkness of the garden.

What is common to all the different kinds of language—abstract, narrative, imagistic—is the plainness of the words. The Passion narrative accounts force us as readers to confront the worst things that can happen to a human being. Betrayal, denial by friends, shame, terror, revulsion from the thought of death, arrest, public humiliation, physical agony, the final, ignominious end of life are presented in the flattest of tones—the flatness contributing to their stark power.

The transactions between the chief priests and Judas are rendered in language that is almost businesslike. When Judas makes the offer of betrayal, the response is, "They were greatly pleased and agreed to give him money." They counter the anguish of Judas' regret, "I have sinned by betraying innocent blood," with the dismissive coldness of "What is that to us, see to it yourself." Even Jesus speaks to him without inflection: "Do quickly what you are about to do."

It is even possible to say that there are comic moments: when the apostles, even as they know Jesus is about to die, are still jockeying for power. Immediately after Jesus informs them that one of them will betray him, they fall to questioning which of them it could be. Then, Luke tells us, "A dispute arose among them as to which of them was to be regarded as the greatest." They still don't get it, the very center of Jesus' message: that it's not about position. Even at this dire moment, he has to run it by them once again: "The kings of the Gentiles lord it over them; and those in authority over them are called benefactors. But not so with you; rather the greatest among you must become like the youngest, and the leader like one who serves. For who is greater, the one who is at the table or the one who serves? Is it not the one at the table? But I am among you as one who serves." Even the event of Peter, or someone, cutting off the ear of the servant of the high priest can be read as a comic moment—particularly in Luke's version when Jesus puts the ear back. At the moment of highest danger, the apostles are still bumblers: Gethsemane's version of Keystone Cops.

THE ORDERING OF THE ROOM for the Passover meal is given much more attention than the Crucifixion. All four Evangelists say simply, "And he was crucified." The Crucifixion, which is a source of a devotionalism that is almost pornographic in its appetite for gory details, is not described with any physical attention in the Gospels. The details of the nails in the hands and feet—so beloved by hellfire preachers, Baroque painters, creators of plastic holy cards, and Mel Gibson—are extra-evangelical. Only John, paradoxically the most metaphysical, the least rooted in the physical of the Evangelists, offers the detail "and there immediately came out blood and water." A shocking and yet austere image: a proof of the totality, the finality of the giving over of a life.

Simplicity, reticence—all that is not embellished, all that in fact might be called minimalist—mark the descriptions of Jesus' sufferings.

THE POWER OF PLAIN LANGUAGE to do the work of solemnity reaches its height in what have been called the Seven Last Words, these words which are not in fact seven words, but seven sentences, spoken by Jesus on the cross. One of them is in the Gospels of Matthew and Mark, three in Luke, and three in John. I present them in the order in which a reader reading the Gospels from page one to the end would encounter them, in order to break into the assumption that they represent a progression, one that comes to an end stop. For me they are best read singly and circularly . . . broken up so that each may be attended to with the proper concentration, with the proper sense of presentness. But, limited by my medium, I cannot enforce the moving circularity I would prefer. I render them, therefore, as I would lines of poetry. Lines that go together to create a lyric, but simultaneously a series of one-line poems, each of which could stand alone.

> *Eli, Eli, lama sabachthani? My God, my God, why hast thou*
> *forsaken me?*
> *Father, forgive them, for they know not what they do.*
> *This day thou shalt be with me in paradise.*
> *Into thy hands I commend my spirit.*
> *Woman, behold thy son, son behold thy mother.*
> *I thirst.*
> *It is finished.*

> *"Eli, Eli, lama sabachthani? My God, my God,*
> *why hast thou forsaken me?"*

THE ONLY SENTENCE Jesus speaks in Matthew's Passion is the "My God, my God, why hast thou forsaken me?" It is in fact a quotation, from Psalm 22. Never has Jesus seemed less divine than when he says these words. If we are meant to believe in the Trinitarian interpretation of the Godhead—Father, Son, and Holy Ghost, all connected by virtue of having only one nature—how is it possible to explain Jesus' radical sense of abandonment? To one of a scholastic temperament, the question might arise: is he abandoning himself?

The words are given in Aramaic first—a strange literalism, as if Matthew were emphasizing the words as words—but they also frame yet another moment of incomprehension. "When some of the bystanders heard it, they said, 'This man is calling for Elijah.'" Their mistake occurs because in Jewish tradition, the pious called upon Elijah to succor them in moments of extremity. "At once one of them ran and got a sponge, filled it with sour wine, put it on a stick, and gave it to him to drink. But the others said, 'Wait, let us see whether Elijah will come to save him.' Then Jesus cried again with a loud voice and breathed his last" (Matthew 27:46–50).

Jesus' abandonment is made more anguishing by the misunderstanding, the bustling of the crowd. His aloneness is public; a mocking crowd witnesses his sense of betrayal, not only by his friends, but by his father, God. His anguish occurs now against the backdrop of busy-ness, of foolish chatter, the rush to offer him something entirely undesired, undesirable: the sour wine he cannot and will not drink—an offering that is perhaps in itself a mockery. His last experience of human activity is the experience of human incomprehension. The clarity of his end—the loud cry, the last breath—is a relief from the unbearable rushing meagerness of what makes up most of human activity. What follows is a natural cataclysm: and at that moment, the very people who were saying, "Let's see if Elijah saves him," seem to be saying, "Truly he was the son of God."

"Father, forgive them, for they know not what they do."

WHAT DOES IT MEAN to forgive people not because they have acknowledged and understood their guilt, but because they never understood what they were doing? This sentiment would seem to be an upending of the ethical demands Jesus made throughout his ministry. If no one knows what he is doing, who is responsible? What is the possibility of responsibility? Where does justice go? Is justice swallowed up by a wave of mercy, whose source may be exhaustion? What are the implications of the abandonment of a category called judgment? Is this the only way the unforgivable can be forgiven? Is this what we want? And how do we understand it in terms of what has gone before? The narrow gate. The parable of the rejected wedding guest, who is banished for failing to have the proper garment. What is truth? What has happened to the demanding judge, separating sheep from goats, casting some into everlasting fire, where there will be weeping and gnashing of teeth? It would seem he has been transformed into the broken man at the point of death, telling us all: Never mind, it's all right, never mind, it doesn't matter.

With these words, the focus shifts; he is not saying that no acts are harmful, but the harm would seem to have no connection to the harmer. There is evil but there are no evildoers. If no one knows what he's doing, no one can be punished. Who would we be, how would we live, if we gave up the possibility of punishment? Of justice? For an exhausted acceptance of the paltriness of what we are.

He enacts for us the greatness of stepping back from what has been inflicted. The refusal of vengeance. Of bitterness. Of, even, the satisfaction of naming properly what has been done.

The grace of "never mind."

Or is it condescension: forget making moral demands on these poor children, they're not up to it?

Who are we, then? How do we live our lives . . . we who do not live always in the last minutes before death?

Do we wish to be called unknowing? Or would we prefer to be held accountable?

Banished to hellfire . . . or forever let off the hook.

Is he seeing something we do not? A vision in which behavior is only a tiny detail in the foreground, like one of the little rabbits playing in the grass in front of the crowned Virgin in a medieval book of hours?

Or are these words apt only at the point of death, another expression of despair, like the expression of abandonment . . . the abandonment now of hope in humans as creatures capable of ethical choice?

How do we live with the possibility that we are incapable of knowledge, therefore of change?

"This day thou shalt be with me in paradise."

AND YET THE GOOD THIEF would seem to have learned something. Jesus is crucified between two common criminals: one curses him, the other rebukes his fellow. "Do you not fear God, since you are under the same sentence of condemnation? And we indeed have been condemned justly, for we are getting what we deserve for our deeds, but this man has done nothing wrong." Then he said, "Jesus, remember me when you come into your kingdom."

There are echoes here of the parable of the Prodigal Son—but the thief is more articulate, his contrition more palpable than the young wastrel's. Once again, though, we are presented with an opulent generosity. A generosity beyond desert. The thief is promised paradise as opposed to heaven. *Paradise.* We hear the suggestion of sensual pleasure rather than the soul's entry into the realm of the noncorporeal. We see the tree of paradise. Color, texture, and scent are evoked, rather than the bliss of the abandoned body.

These words of Jesus are in fact part of a conversation, a dialogue. The partner in the dialogue, known as the Good Thief, speaks and is heard. We are with him as well as with Jesus—part of Jesus' gift to him is the gift of accompaniment. We are with him in the heart-in-the-mouth moment of relief: It's not too late. You're not too late. You made it.

Paradise.

"Into thy hands I commend my spirit."

THIS SHOULD BE THE LAST WORD, but it occurs in Luke, not John, who has the last word, "It is finished." But suppose that this sentence, which is also an echo of the words of a Psalm (Psalm 31), comes before "It is finished." Suppose the final willing comprehension goes before the understanding of completion, of the end. Of the seven words, this is the only one in which Jesus' relation to God seems mutual, loving, secure, not anguished. The only statement of faith. Of Luke's three sentences, this is the one not about forgiveness. It is the peace forgiveness brings. The peace brought by the incomprehensible: for what is more incomprehensible than forgiveness? Commending. Commendable. The letting go.

"Woman, behold thy son, son behold thy mother."

HE COMES LATE TO IT, an acknowledgment of the connection brought about by blood. His treatment of his mother in the Gospels has before this been entirely dismissive. Now at the point of death, his eye falls on his mother, standing at the foot of the cross with one of his disciples. The sight of them calls up in him a new tenderness.

But what is the nature of the tenderness: does it have to do with kinship, with blood? Once again, he is distancing himself from the connection brought about by the accident of animal birth. He does not refer to her as "my mother." He's making an arrangement for a grieving woman, a grieving friend. But the implication of a genetic bond isn't necessary. He is a caretaker, but not necessarily a son. Once again, the importance of the nuclear family is rejected in favor of more open possibilities.

The connection Jesus urges begins with the exhortation to look. "Behold thy son. . . . Behold thy mother." It is the Evangelist who says, "And from that hour the disciple took her into his own home." How strange, the appearance of the word "home." The shelter, the domestic enters. But it was not introduced by Jesus. John introduces it, a surprising appearance at this moment of extremity. These words are followed immediately by the utterly uninflected cry "I thirst."

"I thirst."

THE HOPELESS EXPRESSION of the animal's absurd, humiliating dependence, the contingency of all we are. The desperation of thirst; we cannot live without water. Thirsty, we long for death. Jesus' thirst is unnecessary; he lives in a world in which water could be provided. Instead, he is offered sour wine. On a sponge, a branch of hyssop. He takes it. It doesn't matter. His death will not be forestalled. Drinking the wine, an ineffectual last gesture, he declares, "It is finished."

"It is finished."

OR, IT IS COMPLETED. A formal statement. A statement of understanding. Nothing else to be said.

I COPY THE WORDS OVER: My God, my God, why hast thou forsaken me? Father, forgive them, for they know not what they do; This day thou shalt be with me in paradise; Into thy hands I commend my spirit; Woman, behold thy son, son behold thy mother; I thirst; It is finished. A short paragraph; shorter than the pledge of allegiance, the introduction to the Declaration of Independence, or the preamble to the Constitution.

What words could be plainer than these? The plainness of the language gives me the courage for a plain assertion, an assertion I find it embarrassing to make. But embarrassment is not one of the great emotions, and these words demand the attempt at a response that does not mire itself in self-regard. So now I say: these words are the basis and the foundation of my religious life. They serve for me as a filter, or a funnel, in which everything that has gone before in the Gospels pours itself, and arrives at the end as a pure tincture: clear, usable, entirely free of sediment and residue. The living water. The water of life.

In these words I find the concentrated essence of what I understand to be Jesus' divinity; they are drenched in the human, what the human might be if it were possible to remove from it all the impediments of self-regard, and its fruits, malice, envy, greed. They are a complete articulation of a moment, the moment unto death. The words we can use to describe what they are—words, language, seem too distant, too cold, too abstract. They are utterances. Utterances at the point of death. Utterances without residue: nothing is said that is extraneous. Everything that is needed is expressed. Our fate as speakers—that we are language-making creatures doomed to a failed enterprise—seems to have been bypassed, overcome. These words seem to achieve a complete fit between what is going on and what can be said about it. And they reflect a vision that is entirely sufficient: this is what we need to be seeing and saying if we are to be the best that we humans can be. A saturated consciousness, that takes in the self in all its possibilities: a self in relation to a God, which God is known at that moment as the abandoner, a self in relation to other people, strangers and kin, the deserving and the undeserving. A physical body that lacks what it needs for its continuation. A comprehending mind that marks the form and its completion. The human in relation to the transcendent, the social, the physical, the psychological, the intellectual.

Radical honesty, radical porosity. Language used to obviate the work of language: the naming of differences, of distinctions. Words used to wipe out distinctions, between the good and the bad, those of long attachments and those known for moments only, between the human and the divine.

What is there to say about these words that seem to carry us beyond what can be said? I am discouraged at the prospect; it seems unseemly. I copy and recopy the words. I wish for silence. Then, rather than words, I desire music. I listen to Haydn's *Seven Last Words*, solemnly sweet, harmonious, tragically resigned; James MacMillan's contemporary rendering: anguished, despairing, ending in the ambient silence which Jesus entered as "he breathed his last," said it was finished, gave up the ghost. The *St. Matthew Passion,* before whose sublimity one can only bend the knee.

But it has not been given to me to compose music. Words are what have been given to me. Words upon words.

The Seven Last Words. They are words, but they are unlike other words. Because they are spoken by a character unlike any other, whom we may believe to be divine, whom we have seen speak wisdom, whose personality has impressed itself in a way utterly unique in history. They are not the seven last words of Oedipus or Lear or Alexander the Great or Napoleon or Elizabeth the First or Joan of Arc. They are the seven last words of Jesus. Whose death either has no meaning or creates a meaning unique in the history of the world.

WHAT ARE WE TO DO with these words, how are we to live with them? Particularly since they are not the end of the story. The end of the story is the empty tomb, the Resurrection.

EACH OF THE EVANGELISTS has a story of the Resurrection of Jesus, but as is the case with the death of Jesus, the tones vary greatly. Matthew's is the shortest, and the least emotional. There is not only an angel, but an earthquake doing the angel's work of heavy lifting for him. And Jesus' encounters are not with individuals, but with the disciples as a group.

Matthew uses the event to accuse the Jews of dishonesty and bribery in trying to conceal the story of Jesus' Resurrection. But his main point seems not so much to give a full account of the Resurrection experience, but to use it as a foundational myth for ecclesiastical authority. Jesus' penultimate words are a mandate, "All authority in heaven and on earth has been given to me. Go therefore and make disciples of all nations, baptizing them in the name of the Father, and the Son, and the Holy Spirit, teaching them to obey everything I have commanded you." The last lines almost seem like a throwaway: "And remember, I am with you always, to the end of the age."

Mark's account includes almost no personal interaction between Jesus and any of the disciples; the angel speaks to them, and their response is terror. Many scholars believe that the original version of Mark ends on this moment of terror with the words "and they were afraid." Certainly the last ten verses of this Gospel, which speak of Jesus appearing to the disciples and, echoing Matthew, exhorting them to preach and baptize—in effect, to found the church—seem tonally disjunct, tacked on and perfunctory. "And afterward Jesus himself sent out through them, from east to west, the sacred and imperishable proclamation of eternal salvation."

This "longer ending of Mark," which scholars believe to be substantially stylistically different from all that has gone before, ends with the passage that has been the inspiration for snake handlers: "by using my name they will cast out demons . . . they will pick up snakes in their hands, and if they drink any deadly thing, it will not hurt them." As in Matthew, there is a brief recapitulation of the early ministry of the apostles, their task of spreading the Good News. How different the effect would be if the narrative ended, not with a moment of hopeful forward looking, but with a sense of overwhelmed defeat.

Luke includes the detail of the women bringing spices to anoint Jesus' body, and the unsurprising fact of the apostles' refusal to believe mere women. It is interesting that all the Evangelists present women as the first witnesses to the risen Jesus.

With his usual tenderness, Luke gives the story of the road to Emmaus. Two disciples, grieving and worried about the death of Jesus, meet a stranger on the road. He rebukes them for their lack of faith, then instructs them in the meaning of the Scriptures. They invite him to eat with them. "'Stay with us, because it is almost evening and the day is now nearly over.' So he went in to stay with them." He breaks bread, as he did in the Last Supper, and only then do they recognize him. When they recognize him, he disappears. Luke's version is the most replete with novelistic details; there is the suspense of discovery, the delaying tactic of Scriptural instruction, and the psychological insight "Were not our hearts burning within us while he was talking to us on the road?" And the domestic detail: "he had been made known to them in the breaking of the bread."

When the two disciples are recounting their meeting with Jesus on the road at table, Jesus somehow appears among the disciples. It is in this scene that the greatest case for the corporeal reality of the risen Jesus is made. He insists that he is not a ghost. "Touch me and see, for a ghost does not have flesh and bones, as you see that I have." Most important, he asks for something to eat, and Luke is specific about what is offered and consumed: "They gave him a piece of broiled fish, and he took it and ate in their presence."

Like the other synoptic Evangelists, Luke ends with the post-Resurrection disciples going out and baptizing . . . although, interestingly, Luke's account ends in the temple at Jerusalem, with no hint of a group of disciples unwelcome there, or unwilling to participate in Jewish ritual.

John's version is the most narratively complex of the four, and the source of much of the Midrash that accompanies the story of the Resurrection. Peter and the beloved disciple race each other to the tomb, Jesus is mistaken for the gardener, and Mary is told not to touch him, and Doubting Thomas is made an offer he will not refuse.

Between Mary's first sighting of the empty tomb and her encounter with the risen Jesus, there is the semicomic narrative aside of Peter being outrun by the younger disciple, and the additional delaying tactic of the description of the linen wrappings—both the shroud and the veil that covered his head, and the detail that it was "rolled up in a place by itself." The other disciple, seeing the empty tomb, "saw and believed" . . . but what he believed is not made clear, although the point is that whatever they saw and believed, they didn't understand it.

They return to their homes, and then we rejoin Mary, who is weeping. Her weeping is stressed and restressed. First the two angels at the tomb ask why she is weeping, and she says, "Because they have taken away my Lord and I know not where they have laid him." She sees Jesus, but doesn't recognize him. He asks her two questions: "Why are you weeping? Whom do you seek?" Even after hearing his voice, she doesn't recognize him, "She thought it was the gardener." When she finally recognizes him, it would seem that she reaches out to him, although this gesture is not recorded. He replies harshly—a harshness common in all translations—"Don't hold on to me." "Don't cling to me." "Touch me not."

> *"Who are you looking for?"*
> *She thought it was the gardener.*
> *"Don't touch me."*

Of all sadnesses, we see here the singular sadness of the misapprehension of the beloved. Why did she think he was a gardener? In a rendering of the scene by Rembrandt, he is wearing a straw hat. But he had told them he would rise again. Did none of them, even the most faithful, believe him? Or did grief make her stupid?

I know a cloistered nun who was a movie star before she entered the convent. She was raised in Hollywood and Gary Cooper's daughter was her best friend. When she was a young girl, she went to her new friend's house for the first time. Gary Cooper, among the most famous faces in the world, was watering the lawn in the backyard, wearing only a pair of cut-off jeans. My friend did not recognize him. When she asked for the daughter of the house, Gary Cooper said, "I'll go and get her. I'm the gardener." She said she thinks of that encounter whenever she reads this section of the Gospel of John.

The incorporeality of the risen body. The incorporeality of the image on the screen. The silver screen. When I think of the light of Easter morning, the light of the encounter between Mary and Jesus, it is silver. Fragile light, containing nearly nothing. Heatless, with the residue of night only about to disappear.

I am sure that I have made this up, but it seems to me that when I was a child, Easter was always clear, not warm exactly, but warm enough to wear the new pastel coat, the new hat made of straw, festooned with flowers. Abandoned: the heaviness of winter; taken on: the lightness of first spring. The darkness and wintriness of Lent magically lifted and a new season entered upon: a season of clear light where noon never quite arrived and the thought of sunset was impossible. A light of lightness, where the body, chastened by penitence and grief, gave up its connection with the force of gravity.

A TENDER LIGHT, the light of incorporeality. Does that mean that what Mary saw was image rather than reality? How do we know the difference, except by touch? Why does he not want to be touched? What would be lost by touching, by being touched? "Not until I ascend to the father, to my God and your God." In other words, after I have left the earth forever and you are dead.

In the Oxford English Bible the translation is not "do not touch me," but "do not cling to me." Meaning: be ready at any minute to let me go. It is always a cruel command, "don't cling to me." An accusation of excessive need, excessive demand. But having believed that the beloved was dead, and lost forever, wouldn't the lover want to cling? Is Jesus making the point, at this moment of crisis, that all our loves are transitory, always vulnerable to being overwhelmed by death? That we, creatures trapped in our bodies, trapped in time, must cling to nothing, because everything is always in the process of falling out of our grasp? Is he suggesting that the needs of the beloved to be him- or herself are beyond and greater than the boundaries of the lovers' needs and expectations?

This time when I read the encounter between Jesus and Thomas, I notice something. Thomas never actually touches Jesus. Jesus says to Thomas, "Put your finger here and see my hands. Reach out your hand and put it in my side. Do not doubt but believe." Thomas answers him, "My Lord and my God." We don't see the hand in the wounds, we hear the avowal of faith. The gap seems to me significant. The source of faith is not physical evidence but Jesus' willingness to meet Thomas not where he should be, but where he is.

IT MATTERS TO MANY PEOPLE that the risen Jesus was a physical presence and not a presence experienced so deeply as to make corporeality irrelevant. It does not matter to me. He was able to pass through solid walls; on the other hand, he ate. Fish.

Living as I have done, I would never want to stake my life on the superiority of the corporeal over the imaginary. Otherwise, I would have to believe too much in the superiority of action over language, and too much in the power of death. When children were cruel to me, my mother used to tell me to say to them, "Sticks and stones may break my bones but words will never hurt me." But I could never say that, because I knew it was not only untrue but ridiculous. Oh, I do know that suffering inflicted on the flesh is different from the idea of suffering, and death is death, and I believe that the life that ends in death is ended in all ways that we know. But the importance of the Resurrection is that it says death is not all there is. The point of the Resurrection is the reality of the presence of the beloved dead.

Is it a real presence?

Paraphrasing Pilate, "What is real?"

My father has been dead for more than fifty years. He is beside me now. I can reach out into the air of this room and experience his presence. I do not think that he has burst out of his grave; I do not think that he roams America enfleshed. But he is not dead to me. All the other dead, even those I have loved, are dead to me. He is alive. Because of a love so unlikely, so improbable, so extreme that nothing could stop its flourishing; nothing could cause it to wither or to fade. I do not mistake my father for a gardener. I do not think that he is Jesus Christ. But his death was not the end of his story. His and mine.

Do I believe in a literal resurrection?

I believe in the presence of the beloved after death, a presence that death does not obviate. I believe in memory. I believe, because I have experienced it, a presence that seems so real that one feels breathed upon, touched, fed.

Was the Resurrection real? True?

What is truth?

Is the truth of Napoleon's defeat in Waterloo more true than Lear's night on the heath? Certainly, Lear is more real for me. Is the real the true?

Certainly it is possible.

The importance of the Resurrection is not whether it literally happened but that it insists on the primacy of love over death. That death is not the end of the story. That we may have different stories is, to my mind, neither here nor there.

For me the meaning of the Resurrection is the possibility of possibility.

The great perhaps.

Perhaps: the open-endedness that gives the lie to death.

That opens up the story.

"I dwell in Possibility—
A fairer House than Prose—"

Yet I am a writer of prose, and of necessity prose is my dwelling. Prose, the place where possibilities and impossibilities collide.

"Thou didst choose all that is exceptional, vague and enigmatic."

I am committed to the questions, unsusceptible to final answers.

"Why do you weep?"
"Whom do you seek?"
"Who do you say I am?"

A Note About the Author

Mary Gordon is the author of the novels *Spending, The Company of Women, The Rest of Life, Final Payments, The Other Side,* and *Pearl;* the short-story collections *Temporary Shelter* and *The Stories of Mary Gordon;* and the memoirs *The Shadow Man* and *Circling My Mother.* She has received a Lila Wallace-Reader's Digest Award, a Guggenheim Fellowship, and the 1997 O. Henry Award for best story. She was the winner of the 2007 Story Prize and in 2008 was named New York's State Author. She teaches at Barnard College and lives in New York City.

A Note on the Type

This book was set in Cloister Old Style, a revival of the Venetian types of Nicolas Jenson, designed by Morris Fuller Benton for American Type Founders in 1897.

Nicolas Jenson published his famous *De Praeparatione Evangelica* by Eusebius in 1470 using his roman letter, and it soon became the model for all Venetian type designs.

William Morris patterned his Golden Type on the Jenson type, and the subsequent renewed interest in the letter produced many types based on the Morris model, rather than on the original. Morris Benton (1872–1948), however, chose to go to the source for his design, and bring back the Jenson type in the typeface we today know as Cloister Old Style.